The Rhetoric and Reality of Marketing

An International Managerial Approach

Edited by

Philip J. Kitchen

macmillan

First published 2003 by
PALGRAVE MACMILLAN
Houndmills, Basingstoke, Hampshire RG21 6XS and
175 Fifth Avenue, New York, N.Y. 10010
Companies and representatives throughout the world

PALGRAVE MACMILLAN is the global academic imprint of the Palgrave Macmillan division of St. Martin's Press, LLC and of Palgrave Macmillan Ltd. Macmillan® is a registered trademark in the United States, United Kingdom and other countries. Palgrave is a registered trademark in the European Union and other countries.

ISBN 0–333–98732–2

This book is printed on paper suitable for recycling and made from fully managed and sustained forest sources.

A catalogue record for this book is available from the British Library.

Library of Congress Cataloging-in-Publication Data
The rhetoric and reality of marketing : an international managerial approach / edited by Philip J. Kitchen.
     p. cm.
     Includes bibliographical references and index.
     ISBN 0–333–98732–2
     1. Marketing—Management. 2. Marketing. 3. Marketing—Management—Case studies. 4. Marketing—Case studies. I. Kitchen, Philip J.
     HF5415.13.R454 2003
     658.8—dc21   2002192664

10 9 8 7 6 5 4 3 2 1
12 11 10 09 08 07 06 05 04 03

Printed and bound in Great Britain by
Antony Rowe Ltd, Chippenham and Eastbourne

The Rhetoric and Reality of Marketing

To my wife Diane for her faithful support and companionship during the development, writing and editing of this book. Thank you.

Contents

List of figures

List of tables

Notes on the contributors

Professor Philip J. Kitchen, The Business School, University of Hull, Hull, UK HU6 7RX. Tel: + 44 (0) 1482 466349; Fax: + 44 (0) 1482 346311; email: p.j.kitchen@hull.ac.uk

Philip J. Kitchen, the editor of this book and author of Chapters 1 and 10, holds the Chair in Strategic Marketing at Hull University Business School, Hull University, UK. Prior to this he held the Martin Naughton Chair in Business Strategy, specialising in Marketing, at Queen's University, Belfast, where he founded and directed the Executive MBA programme. At Hull, he teaches and carries out research in marketing management, marketing communications, corporate communications, promotion management and international communications management, and he aims to build an active team of marketing researchers. Before Queen's he was Senior Lecturer in Marketing and Founder and Director of the Research Centre for Corporate and Marketing Communications within the Department of Marketing at Strathclyde University. A graduate of the CNAA (BA[Hons]) initially, he received Master's degrees in Marketing from UMIST (MSc) and Manchester Business School (MBSc) respectively, and his PhD from Keele University. Since 1984 he has been active in teaching and research in the communications domain. He is Founding Editor and now Editor-in-Chief of the *Journal of Marketing Communications* (Routledge Journals, 1995). He has published five books so far, including: *Public Relations: Principles and Practice* (International Thomson, 1997), and *Marketing Communications: Principles and Practice* (1999); *Communicating Globally: An Integrated Marketing Approach* (2000), and *Raising the Corporate Umbrella: Corporate Communications in the 21st Century* (2001), both with Don Schultz of Northwestern University (NTC Business

Books, Chicago, and Palgrave, London). He was co-editor of *Marketing: The Informed Student Guide* (2000), with Tony Proctor (International Thomson).

Dr Kitchen has contributed to such journals as the *Journal of Advertising Research*, the *Journal of Business Ethics*, the *International Journal of Market Research*, the *International Journal of Advertising*, the *Journal of Marketing Management*, the *European Journal of Marketing*, *Marketing Intelligence and Planning*, the *Journal of Marketing Communications*, *ADMAP*, the *Journal of Nonprofit and Public Sector Marketing*, the *International Journal of Bank Marketing*, the *Journal of Corporate Communications*, *Small Business and Enterprise Development*, *Creativity and Innovation Management*; and numerous practitioner journals. Dr Kitchen founded, organised and chaired the 1st International Conference on Marketing and Corporate Communications and was Editor of the Proceedings (Keele, 1996; Strathclyde, 1998). This Conference is now an annual event (Antwerp, Belgium, 1997; Glasgow, Scotland, 1998; Salford, England, 1999; Erasmus Universiteit, The Netherlands, 2000; Queen's, 2001; Antwerp, 2002). Dr Kitchen serves on the Editorial Advisory Board of the *Journal of Marketing Management* and is a Review Board Member for *Marketing Intelligence and Planning* and *Corporate Communications: An International Journal*. He holds Visiting Chair appointments at Massey University, New Zealand, and the School of Management, Rouen University, France.

He has given papers on marketing management, corporate or marketing communications in England, Scotland, the Czech Republic, Estonia, France, Germany, Belgium, Portugal, Australia, New Zealand, Spain, The Republic of Ireland, Northern Ireland, Israel, The Netherlands and the USA.

He is also active in the professional arena. He is a member of the Measurement Academic Advisory Panel (MAAP) with Hill & Knowlton, Inc. (H&K) which involves leading academics from Europe, Pacific Rim and America. This group seeks to bring a robust academic dimension to H&K thinking across a wide range of measurement evaluation tools.

Professor Patrick Hetzel, C/O CIFFOP, Universite Pantheon-Assas, 83 bis, Rue Notre Dame des Champs, 75006, Paris, France; email: hetzel@club-internet.fr

Patrick Hetzel, the author of Chapter 2, is Professor of Marketing at the Panthéon-Assas University in Paris, where he is also Head of the Research Centre in Management Sciences (LARGEPA). He holds a PhD in Management from Jean Moulin University in Lyon. He has published extensively in numerous journals and is a member of Editorial Boards for seven international journals. He is the Editor-in-Chief of *Décisions Marketing*, a journal of the Marketing Association of France.

Dr Martin Evans, Cardiff University, Aberconway Building, Colum Drive, Cardiff CF10 3FU. Tel: +44 (0) 29 2087; Fax: +44 (0) 29 2087 4419; email: mevans16@aol.com

Martin Evans, the author of Chapter 3, is Senior Teaching Fellow at Cardiff Business School. He previously held professorial posts at the Universities of Cardiff, Glamorgan and the University of the West of England. His industrial experience was with Hawker Siddeley and then as a consultant to variety of organisations over 25 years. Martin's specialist research areas include marketing research and information, consumer behaviour and direct marketing. He has over 100 publications including six books, mostly in the aforementioned research areas. He is a Fellow of the Chartered Institute of Marketing (UK). He has received academic prizes for papers presented at the International Marketing Communications Conference, and the Academy of Marketing/Institute of Direct Marketing.

Dr Ioanna Papasolomou-Doukakis, Intercollege Cyprus, 92 Ayias Phylaxeous, Str., PO Box 51604, 3507 Limassol-Cyprus; email: ioanna/doukakis@on2net.co.uk

Ioanna Papasolomou-Doukakis, author of Chapter 4, is an Assistant Professor in the Department of Business at Intercollege Cyprus. Previously she taught and researched at Keele University and Chester Business School in the UK. Dr Doukakis has published papers in the *International Journal of Corporate Communications*, the *Journal of Marketing Management*, the *European Journal of Business Education, Marketing Intelligence and Planning*, and the *Journal of Marketing Communications*. She has contributed chapters and case studies to several academic books as well as numerous papers in conference proceedings. Her research interests include: services marketing management, marketing and corporate communications, internal marketing and marketing management.

Dr Lynne Eagle, College of Business, Massey University at Albany, Private Bag 102-904, North Shore Mail Centre, New Zealand. Tel: +64 9 443 9799 ext: 9455; Fax: +64 9 441 8177; email: l.eagle@massey.ac.nz

Lynne Eagle, the author of Chapter 5, is Senior Lecturer in Marketing at Massey University, Albany Campus, New Zealand. Following a very successful career in advertising, Lynne joined the academic world in 1994. She has since gained a PhD in marketing and become a well-known international researcher in Europe and the Pacific Rim. She has published widely in academic journals in the USA, Europe and the Pacific Rim. Her current interests span marketing, marketing communications, educational training and marketing, and advertising.

Professor Dongjin Yoon, The Management School, University of Korea, Seoul, Korea

Dongjin Yoon, co-author of Chapter 6, is a Professor in the Division of Business Administration at the Woosuk University of Korea where he teaches international business management and strategy. He earned his PhD from the University of Korea. Dr Yoon has worked for Hyundai Corporation and Hyundai Heavy Industries. He also worked at the Korea Institute for Industrial Economics and Trade as a researcher and the POSCO Research Institute as a Senior Consultant. He has published research papers and books on international business management and Korean industries.

Professor Ilchul Kim, School of Media Studies, Dongeui University, Pusan, Korea; email: ickim@dongeui.ac.kr

Ilchul Kim, co-author of Chapter 6, is Professor of Advertising and Public Relations at the School of Media Studies, Dongeui University. Prior to university life, he worked for various companies such as LG (formerly Goldstar), Tupperware Korea and Rexall Korea as Marketing and Promotion Manager, Executive, then President. He received his Master's degree in advertising from Korea University, and his PhD from Hanyang University, Seoul. He has written and translated several books on marketing and communications.

Dr Rosmimah Mohd-Roslin, Bureau of Research and Consultancy, Universiti Teknologi MARA, 40450 Shah Alam, Malaysia. Tel: +603 5544 2097/2093; Fax: +603 5544 2096; email: rosmimah@salam.itm.edu.my

Rosmimah Mohd-Roslin, contributor of Chapter 7, is an Associate Professor at Universiti Teknologi MARA, Malaysia, and is currently the Research Coordinator at the University. She holds a PhD from Keele University, UK, an MBA from Western Illinois University, USA, and a BSc (Marketing) from Indiana University, USA. Her areas of interest include: channels of distribution, channel relationships and retailing as well as relationship marketing. She has published in the *Journal of Global Marketing* and the *Journal of Asia Pacific Business* and presented papers at numerous national and international conferences. She is also the Academic Adviser of the Institute of Marketing Malaysia and she sits on the Editorial Advisory Board of the *Asian Academy of Management Journal*.

Professor Dr Vesselin Blagoev, Managing Director, International University, 169 Evlogi Georgiev Bul, Sofia 1504, Bulgaria. Tel: +359 2 944 1650; Fax: +359 2 943 3337; email: vesco.blagoev@ iu-edu.org

Vesselin Blagoev, the author of Chapter 8, has published seven textbooks and over 40 papers on marketing. He has served as Secretary General of the Council of Ministers, Managing Director of the Privatisation Agency of Bulgaria, President of VECCO, Marketing Director of Electroimpex, among others. He has been a consultant to several dozens of Bulgarian and international companies such as ABB, Intel, Balkantourist, Rila, Bulgartabak, Nina Ricci, Philips Components. Currently he is Professor (Marketing) and Chief Executive Officer of the International University, Sofia. He teaches fundamentals of marketing, marketing management, and innovation management. He has delivered lectures/presentations in the USA, the UK, France, Germany, Holland, Belgium, Austria, Russia, Poland, Japan, Korea, India, Cyprus and elsewhere. He currently serves as Chairman of the Bulgarian Marketing Association. Blagoev is a member of the American Marketing Association and corresponding member of the International Informatisation Academy, Moscow.

Dr Ashish Sadh, Indian Institute of Management (IIMI), Rajendra Nagar, A.B. Road, Indore (M.P.) – 452012, India. Tel: +91 731 32197; Fax: +91 731 321 1050; email: ashish@iimidr.ac.in

Ashish Sadh, co-author of Chapter 9, is as an Assistant Professor of Marketing Management at the Indian Institute of Management,

Indore (IIMI). He received his PhD from Devi Ahilya University, Indore. Previously, he was associated with IIMI as a Fellow, and with the Indian Institute of Management, Ahmedabad as a Research Associate. He has been involved in teaching post-graduate programmes and management development programmes at IIMI. He is involved in many training and consultancy projects conducted for the State Government and for many business organisations. He has published marketing papers in the area of retail banking. His research interests include advertising management, brand management and social marketing.

Ms Sharada Tangirala, #408, Shashi Kiran Apartments, 18th Cross Malleswaram, Bangalore 560055, India. Tel: +91 080 334 6134; email: sharadatangirala@hotmail.com

Sharada Tangirala, co-author of Chapter 9, is a freelance media consultant. She has been associated with several of the leading advertising agencies in India. She has consulted and researched into strategic media planning and buying in J. Walter Thomson, Maa Bozell, McCann Erickson, and Carat in India, and for Carat and Lowe in Sri Lanka. Some major clients include HLL, Unilever (Ceylon), Cadbury, Levis and BPL India. At the time of co-authoring this chapter she was a participant in the International Teachers' Programme for Management Educators, IIM, Indore.

Acknowledgements

With grateful thanks to the contributors, for sharing their knowledge, expertise, understanding and experience within specific countries with the readers of this book. This bringing together of contributors from countries at various stages of economic and social development to share their views on the rhetoric and reality of marketing within their own country is probably without parallel. I am indebted to the contributors who helped clarify the context for this book. Their expertise and cooperation has been invaluable.

I acknowledge, with the contributors, the various individuals, companies and research journals who have assisted us by allowing material to be cited and shared. In addition, we thank the many myriads of marketing students who through their questions and comments have helped the authors sharpen and hone their critical faculties in relation to the marketing discipline. And we also acknowledge the many practitioners and colleagues who, through various means, have influenced development of the thoughts expressed in this book.

To all of you, thank you for your help, guidance, support and encouragement in the expression of these perspectives on the rhetoric and reality of marketing as we move forward into the 21st century.

PHILIP J. KITCHEN

The editor, contributors and publishers are grateful to the following for permission to use copyright material:

Chapter 3: Experian for allowing their material and the GB MOSAIC to be cited; smartFOCUS for allowing their material and their Intelligent Marketing Solutions to be cited;

Chapter 6: Goldstar/LG and Mando for the material cited;

Chapter 7: Mr Syed Nazri and Mr Shukri Yusof from the Impiana Hotel, Kuala Lumpur, and Mr Mohd Azhar from the Urban

Development Authority (UDA) for granting permission and providing valuable assistance in compiling the case materials;

Chapter 9: Mr Anil Thakraney of www.briefonline.com (granted 23 August 2002) for information in appendix 'Generation Next' from the interview (in 2001) with Simon Williams, Chairman, Sterling Group; GCMMF for the information contained in their website www.amul.com given by Jayen Mehta, Group Product Manager, on 11 July 2002; the copyright owner Dinyar to use the Mumbai picture feature on Mumbai Panoramics web site www.geocities.com/mumbai360/, granted 23 July 2002; C. Chakravorty, Joint Director, Data Dissemination for the map of India; HLL for the materials cited as given by Debasis Ray, Corporate Communications Manager, Hindustan Lever Limited; Spectrum Magazines, New Delhi, granted on 26 July 2002 for information featured on www.aandm.com brand diary section for BPL, Close-up, Clinic Plus, Lifebuoy, Pond's, Dettol and Amul. © A&M. All rights reserved throughout the world; Siddharth Sanyal of Dakshinayan, a non-profit, non-religious organization providing basic education and health care to tribal and other rural communities in India (granted 24 July 2002) for pictures of rural India as featured on their web site www.dakshinayan.org, www.linkindia.com/dax.

Every effort has been made to trace all the copyright-holders, but if any have been inadvertently overlooked the publishers will be pleased to make the necessary arrangement at the first opportunity.

List of abbreviations

ACORN	Classification of Residential Neighbourhoods
A-POC	A Piece of Cloth
ASEAN	Association of Southeast Asian Nations
CEO	Chief Executive Officer
CIM	Charted Institute of Marketing
COMECON	Council for Mutual Economic Assistance
CRM	customer relationship management
DMA	Direct Marketing Association
FMCG	fast-moving consumer goods
GCMMF	Gujarat Co-operative Milk Marketing Federation
GDP	gross domestic product
GNP	gross national product
HLL	Hindustan Lever Limited
HMT	Hindustan Machine Tools
HRM	human resource management
IM	internal marketing
IMF	International Monetary Fund
IT	information technology
KCIA	Korean Central Intelligence Agency
LTV	Long Time Value
LVA	Lifetime Value Analysis
OEM	Original equipment manufacturer
PC	personal computer
PR	public relations
R&D	research and development
RFM	Recency, Frequency and Monetary value
ROI	return on investment
VCRs	video cassette recorders

Chapter

Editorial stance on the rhetoric and reality of marketing: an international managerial approach

philip j. kitchen

Aims

This book is intended for practitioners and students who wish to develop an understanding of marketing within specific businesses or industries from eight nation states. In addition to providing a brief overview of marketing, most chapters will explore two case studies; one is a business which adopts what has been termed 'the rhetoric of marketing': that is, a business that proclaims allegiance to the marketing concept, yet for them it never develops much beyond a form of wordplay in which the trappings of marketing are taken for the reality. The other case will explore a business where managers and executives seek to drive marketing deep into the organisational culture and the outcome is the achievement of individual and organisational objectives.

The nation state approach

The book is based on chapters from contributors located in eight countries, ranging from advanced industrial nations such as France and the UK with a high gross national product (GNP) per capita, to a group of nations with developing economies such as Bulgaria and

India. Developed nations are characterised by:

- well-developed infrastructures
- high per capita income
- large-scale industrial diversification
- low rates of population growth
- low rates of economic growth
- a shift in emphasis from manufacturing to service industries

However, developing nations may not share any of these characteristics. Instead, some nation states may have:

- poorly-developed infrastructures
- low per capita income
- small-scale industrial diversification
- high rates of population growth
- medium to low rates of economic growth
- an emphasis on the development of manufacturing industry, or a significant proportion of population employment in agriculture

And, of course, there may be many nation states in between these two ends of the economic spectrum. Thus, in today's world there is no simple dichotomy of developed and underdeveloped nations. Countries cannot be neatly pigeon-holed in this way. For example, in any country that raises its head above the parapet of minimal economic growth, almost immediately multinational corporations make their appearance. Thus, even in countries with very low GNP per capita, we would expect to find examples of business activity where marketing – at least among the multinationals – is taken for granted, and some elements of the marketing concept, however embryonic, can be anticipated. The nation states selected for inclusion in this text are shown in Table 1.1.

When considering expansion into international marketing, often a country's GNP is a good economic starting point. A country's GNP can be a better marker for industrial goods and services than per capita income figures. The reason for choosing per capita income estimation, as in the Table 1.1, is that we are interested in marketing and

Table 1.1 GNP and GNP per capita in selected countries, 2000 (ranked in order of GNP per capita)

Country	GNP $US	GNP per capita $US
France	1,522,060	25,332
UK	1,165,240	19,664
Cyprus	11,400	14,582
New Zealand	48,373	13,217
South Korea	564,371	11,982
Malaysia	102,173	4,575
Bulgaria	9,545	1,193
India	372,272	358

Source: Keegan and Green (1997); figures used are projections

the marketing concept as practised by firms within specific countries, so per capita income figures can be used to estimate demand for products and services deemed attractive by customers and consumers.

However, the figures in Table 1.1 mask certain important facts. A country's GNP or GNP per capita, as stated, is only a beginning. Within specific countries, income distribution can be widely skewed. For example, in India, there is very wide disparity between the upper, the middle and the lower classes. That is why the per capita figure is so low in Table 1.1. The Indian economy is characterised by a triangle with very few at the top and the mass of the one billion population at the bottom. Sometimes, social inequality can be sustained by political and economic will to the detriment of the mass of its population, as in the case of Indonesia today. There is, moreover, a nagging suspicion that many democratic structures in many advanced industrial nations were never designed to assist those at the lowest levels of economic activity. A further inescapable fact is that countries may be at different stages of economic and social development, as depicted in Table 1.2. A further point may be that economic development for some (i.e., rapid economic growth) may be a fairly recent phenomenon in time, whereas for other countries such development may have taken place over a significant time period. Thus, social and cultural development may lag behind economic growth. (Those readers interested in growth opportunities in our eight selected countries can access information from Trade Partners, UK.) Table 1.2, therefore, is only indicative of

Table 1.2 Stages of economic development

Income group by per capita GNP	Countries	Stage of economic development
High-income countries (GNP per capita >$9,386)	France UK Cyprus New Zealand South Korea	Advanced, industrialised, post-industrial
Upper-middle-income countries (GNP per capita > $3,035 but < $9,386)	Malaysia	Industrialising
Low-middle-income countries (GNP per capita > $766 but < $3,035)	Bulgaria	Less developed
Low-income countries (GNP per capita < $766)	India	Pre-industrial

Source: Adapted from Keegan (1999).

potential market development and market opportunity. There is still a significant need to explore market opportunities within individual countries in social and economic distribution terms.

What is the marketing concept?

The marketing approach and concept is taken to be applicable to all types of nations and, *inter alia*, businesses within those nations in terms of managerial attitudes and behaviours. The marketing concept is taken to be managerial commitment to 'satisfying the needs and wants of target customers', to which Kotler (2003) adds 'more effectively and efficiently than the competition'. Undoubtedly, this implies a two-fold balancing act. On the one hand, organisations should 'strive to satisfy customer needs' while, on the other, they also have to 'achieve organisational goals'.

However, a number of questions arise in the context of this book:

1   Is there a difference between proclaimed adherence, and allegiance to the marketing concept in developed and developing nations?

2   Are customer needs satisfied by the products and services offered
    by businesses in countries at different stages of economic devel-
    opment?

3   Are the stages of economic development approach a 'red herring'
    when considering how firms actually *apply* the marketing
    concept?

4   Is there a difference between what the marketing rhetoric
    apparently promises versus what is actually delivered: that is, the
    reality?

5   If there is a difference between rhetoric and reality, where does
    this difference lie?

6   How does this affect overall marketing performance?

7   What effect might a pronounced gap between rhetoric and reality
    have:
    (a)   on consumers?
    (b)   on distributors (or channels)?
    (c)   on competitors?
    (d)   on other publics?
    (e)   on the organisation itself?

The book is designed to tackle these and other questions, and to enable
marketers and students to ponder more deeply on the meaning of
marketing, and how it might be applied in today's world. While these
questions will be raised in each of the chapters, they will be revisited
in the final chapter. Thus here we appeal to marketers (actual or aspir-
ing) who wish to develop knowledge, information and insight in marketing. It is edited, primarily because the application of marketing in
differing cultural contexts requires professional interpretation from
those specific contexts, and not necessarily from an outsider looking
in, and hence the book draws various chapters from recognised experts
in the different countries concerned. Each chapter may be considered
as two case studies accompanied by an overview of marketing in
that cultural context. In each country, two case studies will strive to
illustrate:

■   a business for whom marketing is apparently a form of rhetoric
■   a business where marketing as a concept and business philosophy
    is driven deep into the organisational culture

Is such a book really needed? Marketing as a subject area is riding high on the waves of public, economic and politically popular opinion in the world. There are, admittedly, some doubts being expressed with regard to marketing's bottom-line contribution; equally, very serious reservations are now being expressed about corporate executive greed, even in the face of declining markets. Yet, for now, the concept of 'the market', 'market forces', 'marketing management', 'global marketing' and 'marketing warfare' are common parlance in most nations. But there are also nagging concerns about marketing, especially in the multinational/global arena: perhaps the topic of marketing or the behaviour of firms adopting the concept is indeed open to question, perhaps even deserved criticism. A further concern is that marketing itself may be a metaphor – and perhaps even a poor one – underlying deeper exchange relationships that have yet to be conceptualised more appropriately. A further point seems to be that, despite an ever-increasing crescendo of firms adopting the marketing concept, there is a growing unease among customers and consumers. Are needs really being satisfied? Is marketing more to do with competitive focus than consumer focus? Is marketing more concerned with rhetoric, spin and jargon than actually seeking to satisfy customer needs? Thus, the book, among other things, raises critical theoretical questions, citing issues of current and emergent importance among marketing thinkers.

Is the book for you?

Do you belong to one of the following groups?

1   A practitioner in marketing? A marketing executive, marketing manager, brand manager, market researcher, or in any field associated with marketing as a proclaimed business practice?

2   Associated with a professional organisation such as the Chartered Institute of Marketing (UK), the American Marketing Association, or some other professional marketing association?

3   An undergraduate student studying for a degree in marketing or on a course of study where marketing plays a prominent role?

4   A postgraduate student studying for a direct qualification in marketing (MA, MPhil, MSc) or on a course where marketing is offered as an integral component (i.e., MBA) or as a specialist stream (MA, MPhil, MSc)?

5 A doctoral student in the field of marketing theory or international marketing?

6 Or are you, like me, simply concerned about what marketing is now, what it claims to be, or its relevance to businesses and consumers in the 21st century?

If the answer is 'yes' to any of the above questions, then you simply must read this book!

Genesis and excursus of this book

The origin of any book, even one that is edited, has to come from some spark of creativity. In this case, my thinking on the subject of marketing was stimulated by the same issues that characterise the genesis of *The Future of Marketing* (see Kitchen, 2003):

1 Direct involvement as a teacher and researcher in the domain of marketing for nearly two decades.

2 Continuous reading in the subject area: the attempt to understand what marketing is, what it was, where it stands now as a theoretical and practical discipline, and how and in what ways it may develop in the future.

3 Association with many colleagues and students who have stimulated me by their company, and their critical comments, amid the on-going swirl of academic activity in the marketing discipline. As an aside here, sometimes we are so busy in the teaching or practice of marketing that we have no time to examine the actual meaning of the discipline whose principles we espouse.

I cannot avoid the feeling that there is something amiss in the current state of marketing. Here, I offer two analogous metaphors. The first is derived from Wroe Alderson's early writings, which are beginning to be appreciated for his insights into what marketing was and what it may become (for readers interested in this, there are many references in Sheth, Gardner and Garrett, 1988). In an early paper, Alderson (1964) likened marketing to biological entities:

> The best analogy for the capacity of a system to survive is the health of a biological organism ... it is rational to exercise proper care to keep the body or the

system healthy. The prime strategy is a … strategy of avoidance. The individual tries to avoid infection or other conditions that might cause illness. Through occasional medical examinations he hopes for early detection of what might otherwise become an incurable and otherwise fatal disease. The executive watches for maladjustment in the system and attempts to provide prompt remedies. *Above all, he should try to prevent the system from falling into the condition that has been called the extinction mode.* (Alderson, 1964; italics added)

Marketing itself can be seen as a system with sets of rules, norms, values, definitions, models and approaches. In my other book (Kitchen, 2003), several authors identify serious health problems with the system known as marketing. One author, Michael Thomas, states that the marketing profession (at least in its academic ranks) is suffering from *epistemopathology*, or the application of 'diseased, sick, and bad knowledge that is mechanistically applied to contemporary global market systems, in self-serving ways, to identify and solve immediate problems, problems which are not well understood, and without any consideration of the ripple effects on society as a whole'. Evidently, parts of marketing may be ill or diseased, and may be in need of remedial attention. Among other things, therefore, this book is a clarion call to all involved with the discipline – either practically or as teachers – to understand the conceptual rock on which marketing is founded, and to help strengthen and indeed renew the foundations.

The second analogous metaphor is derived from Loren Eiseley, a 20th-century anthropologist, naturalist, humanist and poet. He was a prolific writer, with many books and hundreds of articles to his credit. In *The Star Thrower*, we find the following:

Legend has it that in some remote castle on the Continent, two intertwined stairs run upward in a tower. So clever was the architect, so remarkable was his design for the stairway, that although the steps twine and intertwine in their ascent, a man ascending gets no glimpse of his counterpart coming down. Both are private pathways. (Eiseley, 1978)

Admittedly, Eiseley used this metaphor in an anthropological sense, where man either dragged himself upwards from the elementary slime from whence he came, or trudged continually downwards in a movement away from innocence and perfection. Now, moving this metaphor away from its anthropological moorings, surely many marketers (myself included) have wondered about the current nature and status of marketing?

On the one hand, the marketing concept would appear to offer an ideal rationale for satisfying (or at least attempting to satisfy) customers and their needs while simultaneously satisfying the organisational imperative for sales, profits, growth, and market, mind and heart shares. Of course, this has now to be accomplished in the visibly rarefied atmosphere of social responsibility, or 'good corporate citizenship'. Straight away, in the train of the marketing concept comes the whole associated processual baggage of analysis, planning, implementation and control. Yes, we know all this; it has been taught, repeated and echoed in multitudinous books and journals, all having, if not the ring of veracity, at least a common chord of crescendoed chorus.

Yet, on the other hand, there is growing unease, a growing disquietude that perhaps organisations are far more focused on their own needs, profits, sales and so forth than they are on customers. Many customers and consumers are becoming dissatisfied not only with products and services, but also with firms who proclaim benefits ostensibly in the name of customers and consumers, but whose real purpose is to improve organisational efficiencies and scales of economy, while simultaneously creating ever greater barriers between themselves and their customers.

There is also a very real and related problem – admittedly not entirely within the province of marketing – that the sight of executives wallowing in the trough of corporate greed is in fact nauseating and obnoxious to many observers. Moreover, the vaunted and yet muted appeal of President George W. Bush (9 July 2002) to corporations to act ethically and with social responsibility initially lacked the needed teeth to bring recaltricant corporations and greedy executives to heel. It is difficult for executives to heed this voice of caution, especially when new cans of pleasurable swill arrive so regularly at the trough.

Loren Eiseley's metaphor can be likened to marketing typologies. One type of marketing is like the man making his way upwards on the staircase. Through the long slow developmental process of product, production, sales, marketing and societal orientation some corporations do indeed display social responsibility, they are good corporate citizens, they reach out to customers and consumers and they try to value their customers' needs and the concomitant delivery of desired satisfactions at every organisational level. They drive the marketing concept deep into every level of organisational culture. Here, in this text, we will see attempts by organisations to do this: they reap the rewards one would expect. But there is still a process involved which needs to be consistent, on-going and iterative, not forgotten or discarded.

Another type of marketing can be likened to a man making his way downwards on the staircase. Here, corporations have lost their initial marketing impetus. They perhaps started with at least a desire to satisfy customers and their needs. They developed good products and good services; they reached out and built real relationships. Customers invariably rewarded such efforts with their patronage. But perhaps marketing efforts, just like the products that are sold, have become adulterated. The last ounce of profit has to be squeezed from the product, the packaging, the communications and the distribution. Something of value is inexorably lost in this type of process. Marketing reality has been stripped away to the point where marketing has become a form of rhetoric, and where words have replaced reality as the dominant paradigm.

An in-between example is where a business practises 'real marketing at home', and a form of arrogant 'marketing imperialism abroad'. Problems arise when shameful marketing-related tactics abroad impact on the core business at home.

It would be easy to conclude that that is the end of Eiseley's metaphor, but it is not. Instead, the two forms of marketing – and all the shades in between – are inextricably interwoven. In the marketing discipline, the two staircases do cross over and interact, and at any point in our hustle to get to the top we may pass others on the way up, or others who, having failed to ascend to the heights, settle for rhetorical equivalence. And there are at least two further issues to contend with.

Let us suppose that on some landing in our metaphorical staircase there is a large mirror. I wonder whether it is not worth pausing occasionally, not to check the straightness of the tie, or the brightness of the boots, but simply to see who we are, and what we are doing in this place? What is our contribution to this marketing discipline? What do we really stand for?

The second issue concerns the tower itself. Surely, we cannot just be concerned with our progress or otherwise on the stairs? Outside the tower the whole world of economic, political, social, cultural and philosophical thought rushes on. Surely we as marketers need to be involved here as well?

As we now move into the 21st century, we require not just to observe the old time-worn (I was going to say time-honoured, but perhaps that is inappropriate) materials of marketing but we must be willing to embrace new mind sets and new behaviours. There are many significant barriers that still have to be overcome. Derived from an earlier context (see Kitchen and Schultz, 2001), these problems and barriers can be stated as shown below.

1   The marketing world requires new developmental paths for marketers at all organisational levels (but remember to think outside our own specific staircase).

2   Marketers must now balance marketplaces with marketspaces.

3   Organisational constraints must be recognised as such, and overcome over time (always with consumer needs in mind).

4   A research-rich consumer understanding is vital, not just derived from macro environmental criteria.

5   Both marketing communications *and* corporate communications are needed to compete effectively in today's crowded and turbulent environs.

6   Marketing training is required at *all* organisational levels.

7   Mind maps – ways of seeing the marketing world – may need revisiting, reviewing, and re-adjusting to reflect current developments.

8   Mind maps to see what the world outside our narrow disciplinary constraints *thinks of marketing* are worthy of our attention.

The final strand of 'genesis' took place in 2001. Each year, the Academy of Marketing (formerly the 'Marketing Education Group') organises a conference. For the first time, however, the Marketing and Strategy Group at Cardiff University organised an accompanying 'research event' titled as 'In Search of Excellence for Research in Marketing'. The purpose of the event, which is now held annually, is to 'examine effective ways of stimulating scholarly research in marketing of international excellence [within the UK]'. I find attendance at this event to be personally worthwhile. It serves to stimulate the grey matter concerning what marketing might be, has been, and where the discipline is headed, since there is indeed a problem with marketing in the UK and many other countries, which is that despite all the teaching, writing, instruction, and training given now over 30 or more years, so many firms are *bad at marketing*. In the UK, more consumers and customers are provided with lower-quality products, with higher than average prices and with poorer services than in any other country I know. Virtually any comparison of any product category in the UK with others (even if we just compare with the USA or another European nation) reveals significant shortcomings and a pronounced lack of ability to satisfy customer needs. So, even as academics pronounce the virtues of an American-led marketing concept in lecture theatres, and as marketing managers polish their trappings of marketing, the substance of marketing seems to evade or escape attention. Of course, whether this is the case in the eight countries and at least 16 case studies in this book remains to be seen; but at least this book is one (albeit small) attempt to address some of the issues involved.

The content of the book

I have been pleased that several marketing writers have provided a contribution for this book. These writers were invited arbitrarily by me to submit a chapter from the viewpoint of eight different nation states. I knew of their personal interest in the development of marketing as a global topic, and in terms of its application in their own national (sometimes international) contexts. However, as stated above, they are not the only people speaking on and writing about marketing. Readers will note I have deliberately left out the USA (often seen as the world's leading economy) from this book. This is because so much of our marketing thought and terminology comes from that country. The question often not asked, however, is the extent to which such thought can be translated into recognisably beneficial marketing actions in other countries around the world? Very few writers seem to question the relevance and applicability of the marketing concept in other nation states. There are exceptions.

Behind the contributors of the chapters in this book are many other people (see, for example, Arndt, 1976; Baker, 1999; Cox *et al.*, 1964; Day and Wensley, 1983; Dholakia and Arndt, 1985; Firat, Dholakia and Bagozzi, 1987; Fullerton, 1987; Hunt, 1983, 1991, 1992; Levitt, 1960; Shapiro and Walle, 1987; Zinkhan and Herscheim, 1992) who have helped shape the world of marketing as we know it today. However, as will be seen within the chapters that follow, that world of *shaping* is still going on, both from this contribution and those that follow.

Conclusion

Let me now extricate the editorial voice from the chapters that follow. Apart from some minor stylistic interventions and the necessary focus on rhetoric versus reality, readers will hear from the authors themselves. The chapters are tackled in GNP per capita order, which means that chapters are taken from:

- France
- the UK
- Cyprus
- New Zealand
- South Korea
- Malaysia
- Bulgaria
- India

All the authors consider marketing from their own country context and provide at least two illustrative cases of how marketing is practically applied in the countries concerned. I prefer to think of these chapters as encountering individual minds in the process of reflection on our discipline. I hope that readers will enjoy the encounters; I know I have. As readers now set out on their journey of discovery, I will be walking alongside. We will meet again in the final chapter.

The rhetoric and reality of marketing in France

patrick hetzel

Aims

Modern marketing practices were implemented in French firms during the 1960s, or at least a decade after implementation started to be taken seriously in the USA. This delay can be explained not only by the specific market context in France but also by the fact that some employees were reluctant to adopt a strong customer orientation within their firms. Here, the marketing rhetoric was literally then *the rhetoric* of their management. This is developed in the first section of the chapter. The second section explores the case of Rodier, a French fashion brand manufacturer who tried to implement a strong marketing concept but finally failed because global customer satisfaction could not be achieved, and targeted customers who purchased once did not come back again. The last section of the chapter uses the case of 'A-POC', another fashion brand launched by the fashion designer Issey Miyake who has a strong presence in France, where his world-wide 'couture' headquarters is located. This launch was a success because the firm was able to create a strong and real (at least it was perceived by the customer as such) link between the customers and the organisation, which was indicative of a strong marketing orientation. Despite these examples of firms proclaiming allegiance to the marketing concept, France still seems somewhat apart from most other developed industrialised nations. On the other hand, some ethical issues concerning marketing rhetoric and reality are undoubtedly bringing the country closer to the marketing practices adopted by businesses in many other industrialised nations around the world.

Introduction

France is undoubtedly a country in which marketing concepts and practices were mainly considered, developed and implemented after the Second World War, as indeed was the case in many European nations. Nonetheless, it has already been established that some marketing techniques were already being used in France at the start of the 20th century, for example, in the automotive industry (see Fridenson, 1981; Hetzel, 1999). It would be presumptuous to say that the present chapter will provide an exhaustive view of the rhetoric and reality of marketing since those early days in France. Instead, my goal is to show that, over time, marketing has become (in most French companies) a very widespread and influential concept. Nonetheless, the way it has been applied still allows scope for differentiation between marketing practices between firms. After an overall consideration of the marketing concept in France which will allow exploration of the view that some aspects of marketing remain specific to France, this chapter will use two case studies taken from the French fashion industry in order to indicate two dimensions: on the one hand, how a business in France has adopted the rhetoric of marketing without translating this into delivering customer satisfaction (the Rodier brand); and, on the other hand, how a second business in France has delivered the concept of marketing via development of a strong brand strategy (the A-POC concept of Issey Miyake) and thereby brought it into being.

The reason these cases are derived from the French fashion industry is because they accurately display the differences between the marketing concept as a form of rhetoric and as reality, and also because fashion itself is a significant industry that has strong resonance for both French culture and for the French economy (Hetzel, 1998). The chapter will discuss the following areas:

- the marketing concept in France

- the consequences of adopting marketing as a form of rhetoric: the case of Rodier France over the last decade

- the outcome of driving marketing deep into the culture of an organisation (namely, the A-POC concept of fashion designer Issey Miyake) or, put another way, how customers can become designers of their own fashions

- summary and conclusion

The marketing concept in France

The use of the English word 'marketing' by French executives commenced during the 1950s. Then, it concerned descriptions of 'avant-garde' market practices and techniques in the US. Consequently, the meanings of marketing and related ideas were ambiguous in the sense that such words cannot be expressed easily by words in the French language, as there are no direct equivalents (Meuleau, 1988). It was only at the start of the 1960s that the marketing concept was really implemented by French firms in order to stimulate the home market, and a few years later the international market. The first companies that systematically implemented the department era of marketing were large French corporations, for example, Peugeot and Renault in the automotive industry (Lévy-Leboyer, 1980). This relatively recent development of marketing, compared to the much longer history of capitalism in France (which can be traced back to well before the 19th century) explains why, at the beginning of the 21st century, when French executives speak about 'marketing', they often define it as a real 'revolution' in terms of actual business practice. It is argued therefore, that there are two eras in French business history: a pre-marketing era and a marketing era. Most of the time, implementation of the marketing concept by business pioneers or leaders is accompanied by an increase in the market shares of those companies which, in other words, means that nowadays in France, marketing implementation is seen as inevitable by marketing managers, senior executives and even by non-marketing executives.

The level of marketing development of French companies can be studied via several criteria.

1 The rhetoric of marketing: how strongly does the company take into consideration the customer as its central focus? Is this seen as just a form of discourse, or can its application be plainly perceived, inside and outside the organisation?

2 The existence of a marketing department, and whether it is conjoint or separate from sales within the organisation.

3 The existence of levels of control that allow the firm to make sure that what is promised to customers or potential customers can be provided effectively by the firm.

In summary, the firm has to do its best to reduce differences between customer expectations (especially if the firm has created these expectations via a form of marketing) and what the customers actually receive.

Without hesitation, in contemporary France, marketing is part of business reality and the marketing prowess and efficiency of successful firms known throughout the world, such as Michelin, L'Oréal, Danone, Louis Vuitton, Chanel, Renault or Sofitel, are indicative of this. But on the other hand, this does not mean that the whole picture is positive. France has some cultural specifics that should not be ignored and, in some cases, they can have severe consequences on marketing reality. To give a good description of this national specific context, we have to return to the 1950s. After the Second World War, the French state played a key role in economic development and the country is one of those within the EU which has, together with the Scandinavian countries, the strongest level of taxation. As a consequence of this, the country and its consumers still live in a culture of a 'provident welfare state'. France is also a country in which, until very recently, the influence of the Communist Party was very strong, especially because of its links with workers' unions. As a matter of fact, the 'class struggle' is still a shared vision of the world for some workers and employees in France. This means that, even now, it is sometimes very difficult to establish a customer-oriented vision within a French firm and make sure that this vision will be shared by most employees. Some employees still make a strong connection between the rhetoric of marketing and capitalistic rhetoric. Marketing, for some, can be seen to be the discourse of the ruling class.

Simultaneously, and adding to the cultural soup in which marketing exists, top and middle management have been educated by the *grandes écoles* system or the university system (Hetzel, 2000) and most of these executives and managers have been exposed to marketing concepts, if not to a strong marketing education. Therefore many are convinced of the fact that marketing allows firms to establish and maintain a competitive advantage in the market. For this reason, most managers and executives usually want to implement the marketing concept and practice within their firms; but sometimes, especially in service industries, employees associate customer orientation with a trick used by the management in order to stimulate them and obtain better productivity. Those who have travelled to France as tourists can usually tell stories about bad service experiences in some

Parisian restaurants or shops. Compared to some other developed industrialised nations, France is a country in which the difference between the rhetoric and reality of marketing is still a very strong issue, mainly (but not only) in the service industries. This is largely because it does take significant investment of time and training to convince employees who are in contact with customers how important it is that they provide customer satisfaction. Implementing a marketing vision that will be shared by all within every firm therefore remains a challenge in France. Fortunately, the globalisation of the French economy has contributed to reducing the gap between France and other G8 member countries.

Another aspect that cannot be ignored about France and marketing is the existence of a paradox. Even if, as previously explained, some employees of French firms are still reluctant to become customer-oriented and try to avoid marketing, the level of marketing knowledge of French customers (and, of course, some of those customers are also employed by French firms) has increased significantly over the last decades. France even has several television shows (e.g., one called 'Capital' and another called 'Culture Pub') which explain marketing and communication strategies to their audiences. More and more customers are aware of marketing strategies and have a very high level of understanding about what firms are doing in order to retain existing customers or attract new ones. As a consequence, expectation levels of customers are becoming higher and higher. More and more customers are analysing firm strategies and are making direct linkages between what a firm promises (its rhetoric) and its actual behaviour. This type of linkage, for example, contributed to a very strong boycott of all Danone products at the beginning of 2001 in France. In fact this firm, which is very proactive regarding marketing and has a very good image on the French market because of its customer and humanistic orientation, was suspected of secretly developing a massive downsizing operation. For many French customers, there was a contradiction between the proclaimed positive image of the firm and the very negative imagery associated with this specific behaviour. Customers noticed a difference between the rhetoric and the behaviour of the firm. Because the firm had developed a very strong level of ethical expectations, it became difficult for the customers to understand that the firm was not dealing ethically with its own human resources.

More and more firms are seen as one single entity and therefore it becomes impossible to separate the various aspects of its economic behaviour. Simply delivering a form of rhetoric does not cut much ice in today's marketplace (Hetzel, 1996). Customers are evaluating firms globally. Specific situations leads customers to make links between marketing and business ethics. Without any doubt, this issue has become an inevitable dimension of marketing practice in contemporary France (Pras, 1999).

The consequences of adopting marketing as a form of rhetoric: the case of Rodier France

Rodier is a brand that became famous during the 1960s in France. The firm was part of the French fashion industry and specialised in designing, producing and selling clothes for women. The brand was one of the first in the fashion industry in France to develop distribution strategy via franchising and was targeting middle-class working women between the ages of 25 and 50. From the 1960s to the 1990s, the firm built a strong brand that was well appreciated by targeted customers and they progressively opened a chain of 300 shops all over France, reaching a total turnover of approximately FF600 million by the end of the 1990s. Even during the years of the textile crisis (mainly the 1980s), the company was able to maintain its position in the French market. This was not always the case among its national competitors. French brands in the fashion market were challenged more and more by brands from other EU countries (mainly Italy and Spain), or even from companies that did not produce the products themselves, concentrating their efforts on design and sales (the production being done by subcontractors outside the EU). But at the beginning of the 1990s, Rodier had to develop a new strategy in order to maintain its global turnover which was slowly but inexorably decreasing. The main reason that pushed the senior and marketing management to define a new strategy was the fact that the customers who were very loyal to the brand, and who had purchased the brand 30 years ago, were of course no longer aged between 25 and 50 but were now between 55 and 80. The problem the brand faced was the ageing of its customer base. In order to survive, the brand had to attract and retain younger customers. To do so, the company decided to carry out an extensive market research exercise in order to understand the needs of active French women aged between 30 and 50. Once the data were collected and analysed, management decided to develop an entirely new marketing concept with a new marketing mix. Within the elements of the mix, the firm decided to invest strongly in two components: new product design and a strong advertising campaign using the slogan: 'J'assure en Rodier' ('With Rodier, I can be sure').

The purpose of the 'revised' marketing concept was to be able to attract and retain younger women. In other words, with the same brand, the aim was to gain the custom of those younger customers. Some competitors of the brand, such as Devernois, decided to go in a different direction. On the one hand, they recognised that it would be difficult for Rodier to modify entirely the image of the brand, and on the other they considered that women aged between 50 and 70 would also have some fashion needs, so Devernois simply decided to target that specific age group instead of targeting a younger clientele as Rodier were doing. The scene was thus set for a disastrous marketing outcome. But there was more to come …

However, the advertising campaign by Rodier was very successful: it was seen by most of the women the firm were targeting and many decided to go to the Rodier shops in order to see the new products. But the strong communication rhetoric that was omnipresent in the advertising campaign and supported by the new product designs was not discernible in the retail outlets in terms of their style and layout. Most of the stores, being franchise outlets, had not been renovated. The new and trendy products thus did not have the same strong impact they had during the market test period when they were displayed in very attractive scenarios. Rodier had apparently applied the marketing concept, and underpinned it with market evidence, so their impact on the market could have been strong; but they had neglected the fact that it would take some time to renovate the shops. They were not directly owned by the firm and therefore Rodier had to negotiate renovations shop by shop with the owners. By the time most of shops were renovated, the customers had already departed to pastures and fashions new. The brand thus was able to attract new prospective customers, but because these could not immediately find the environment they were expecting, dissatisfaction was high.

This shows that having a good concept is insufficient. A brand has to make sure that the concept is translatable in good time in all the aspects of the marketing mix and perceived as such by the targeted customers, otherwise the risk of failure becomes very high: this is exactly what happened to Rodier France. And yet this is also an example of the rhetoric of marketing being frustrated by failure of management to follow through with the necessary realities encountered at the point of sale.

What often makes it quite complex to develop an efficient marketing concept and bring it into reality is the fact that between the firm and its (potential) customers, one element of marketing (in this case, distribution) can play a key role. A marketing strategy can be very sophisticated, but if it is neglecting the role that distribution plays in the *mise-en-scène* of the whole marketing concept, it can very easily fail. It is important to note that the case of Rodier is by no means unique in France. A number of French firms who have either developed a new concept or launched a new product have had to face this specific reality. This reality is even stronger when the firm has to deal with very strong French distribution firms such as Carrefour, Auchan or Leclerc, which have the dominant market shares and will fight like tigers to retain them.

In the case of Rodier, it was insufficient just to recognise problems, even where this was underpinned by research data. Changing product lines and announcing such changes by means of advertising smacks of product and sales orientation. This is evident in the failure of Rodier to consider customer reactions, as in the case of offering new wine in old bottles (i.e., new brands in the same old distribution outlets), but also in their failure to anticipate likely competitive response. Thus at the same time as they failed to attract new customers by insufficiently incorporating their needs and requirements in terms of store ambience, their existing customer base was put off by Rodier's strategy, and simultaneously were attracted by a firm who were clearly targeting their needs. Thus, rhetoric alone is insufficient; instead marketing efforts must be thought through and planned for at every level and contact point of the customer interface.

Driving marketing deep into organisational culture: the A-POC concept of fashion designer Issey Miyake (or, put another way, how customers can become designers of their own fashions)

This section of the chapter explores the case of 'A-POC', a fashion brand launched by designer Issey Miyake who is strongly present in France, where his world-wide 'couture' headquarters are located. This launch was a success because the firm was able to create a strong and real (or at least perceived by the customer as such) link between the customers and the firm. This case will show how the marketing concept can be translated from a form of rhetoric to a reality that can be perceived as such by customers. Here, instead of simply providing a description of the firm strategy, we have chosen to develop a 'romanticised' version of what really happened to a customer (Isabelle) who is already accustomed to the Miyake brand and who discovered the new concept of the designer, 'A-POC'. The material recounted here is derived from qualitative data collected by the author. It allows for a demonstration of how a company (brand) can link the rhetoric with the reality (or at least the one perceived by the customer).

Isabelle is a 35 year old executive, working at a Parisian advertising agency located in the 'Triangle d'Or' of Paris, an area of the city that has a very important concentration of luxury brands and shops. She is single and lives in the Marais, a very 'trendy' area of Paris. Every morning, when she goes to her office, she walks past the Christian Dior and the Thierry Mugler boutiques. Very often, she has the same kind of thoughts about those brands: 'They are very conventional and easy to interpret.' Being a real 'Bobo' (this means 'Bourgeois-Bohème', as described by Brooks, 2000) type, she prefers more trendy brands and her colleagues consider her a victim of fashion. She is looking for brands which attempt to portray a sophisticated discourse, with a strong intellectual emphasis, for brands that are not known by every one, with a strong image, but only within a small select group of people.

Therefore, one of her favourite fashion designers is Issey Miyake. Born in 1935 in Hiroshima, he studied graphic design. He started his career in *haute couture* companies such as Guy Laroche and Hubert de Givenchy in Paris and rounded out his apprenticeship time in the employ of Geoffrey Beene in New York City. In 1970, he returned to Japan to found Miyake Design Studio. Today, this couture activity is located in France. Though much of his work has an undeniable tie to the silhouettes and materials of traditional Japanese clothing, Issey Miyake has sought to create a new style that is both multi- and meta-cultural. Throughout his career he has attempted to create design truths and that is exactly why Isabelle likes his work so much. He is a real intellectual who tries to create a new kind of relationship between consumers and his brand.

Issey Miyake is probably best known for 'Pleats Please', an on-going line of clothing established in 1990; Isabelle's closet is full of products which come from that specific brand of the designer.

She has been collecting the products since the brand was launched and does not want to give away any piece. She is very proud to wear, from time to time, some clothes from the Issey Miyake Pleats Please collection which are 10 years old. A lot of people around her at work notice that she has a very unique style of dressing and make some very nice comments about her clothes. This is part of her identity. But what she appreciates probably the most is that only she knows how expensive the clothes are because only fashion insiders are able to notice that her clothes were created by Miyake. When people wear Chanel or Gucci, everyone can tell that those clothes are expensive, but the geometrically shaped garments that become the basis for tight Fortuny pleats do give a unique appearance. In the Miyake collection, the fabrics are usually not patterned, allowing the light and dark shades created by the pleated surface to take precedence. While the overall effect may sound severe, it is in fact the opposite. Remarkably, clothing from Pleats Please collections is also relaxed and elegant, and this image is exactly what Isabelle is looking for. In some cases, when the geometric base shape of a piece is more elaborate, the resulting form has an organic sort of complexity, but does not lose its approachability. Miyake is a brand for those who have a very strong fashion culture. The products are not easy to access; they also convey a very specific semiological content.

More recently, Issey Miyake created a new brand, 'A-POC' (A Piece of Cloth), which empowers the wearer to become the designer. This remarkable collection is based on yardage of cloth which has been woven in such a way that the complete article of clothing, ready to be cut, breaks in the weave in a yardage matrix. At the autumn 1999 catwalk show (Isabelle being a very good customer, she was of course invited), Miyake presented the design process as theatre. Standing on the runway with a model in a long-sleeved, hooded floor-length gown, he took a pair of scissors to the outfit before an astounded audience and proceeded to alter it into an entirely different ensemble. Models also presented the work uncut as long banners, glorifying the fabric itself. The show was a dramatic expression of the tenets of Miyake's design philosophy of individuality in the context of universality.

A few weeks later (February 2000 in Tokyo), Issey Miyake opened his first A-POC shop and a second shop was opened in Paris in September 2000. This Parisian shop was opened in the Marais area where Isabelle lives, which reinforced her identification process with the brand. This location expresses the clear desire of the designer to attract an intellectual, avant-garde customer more capable of appreciating his work than the traditional French 'golden mile' on the Faubourg Saint Honoré.

Isabelle was also invited to the opening ceremony of the shop. Situated on a corner, the shop lies in a heavy pedestrian traffic zone. On the day of the opening, the mobs of guests were so thick that visitors could not fit on to the pavement and were forced to walk down the middle of the street. Upon approaching the shop, Isabelle was immediately aware of the stark contrast of the bright white light of the interior when compared to the relative darkness of the narrow street. The façade along the street is lined with milk-white windows, which allow not even a glimpse of the interior. This air of mystery intrigues while the guests inside experience the wall as a gift of privacy and testimony to their belonging to the 'happy few' of the Miyake tribe.

That evening, the store is full of Issey Miyake connoisseurs. Isabelle already knows some of them because they meet at least twice a year when the company organises fashion shows in Paris. She feels as if she belongs to a secret society with its specific codes of aesthetic and rituals of adoration. Isabelle knows everything about Issey Miyake's life, his collections and his philosophy. Such an event is a good opportunity to approach the designer and to experience something unique. In the middle of the store, Issey Miyake is introducing the Bouroullec Brothers to other guests. They are the architects who worked on the store and its interior design. Ronan Bouroullec says a few words to the audience:

> We were not given restricted specifications about the functioning, capacity, the materials, or even the colour scheme of the boutique. Nevertheless we were to follow a concept: to recreate the atmosphere of a workshop, a tailor's atelier, as Issey Miyake considers that A-POC is in perpetual evolution. We therefore worked on the idea of flexibility in such a way as to be able to adapt the boutique to the evolving concept.

And Issey Miyake also adds a few words:

> Dear friends, all you need are scissors. With this new brand I wanted to create a new relationship between you and my work. When I was conceptualising this new collection, I was thinking about our conjoint relationship. Who is the designer? You or me? Now you know, the answer is: you AND me. Hereby, I wanted to signify the fact that we are all fashion designers and fashion wearers. By using scissors, you are becoming tailors of a conjoint creation process. I hope

that I will learn a lot from you and that I will see my products in forms that I did
not even imagine myself or expect.

Isabelle is very enthusiastic about what she hears and sees. She
feels very proud that her ten-year loyalty to the fashion designer
enables her to be part of a small tribe of trendsetters. When she
returns home that evening, she has the following thought: 'I am so
happy to have this secret garden, this very unique relationship with
Issey Miyake. This brings some sunshine into my everyday life and
it allows me to escape from the massive nature of our contemporary
consumption.'

A marketing concept, in order to be brought into reality, has to be
strongly perceived by the customers that are targeted and must
clearly take into consideration their specific needs and desires. This
is exactly what A-POC is doing. The brand is building up a new kind
of relationship between the customer and the designer. Everything
possible is done, with the several elements of marketing mix (the
product, the price, the location and the sales area design and advertising), to make sure that the customer will feel treated as someone
unique, *and different from the others*. Bringing customisation into
reality is part of the success of the whole concept.

Summary and conclusion

In this chapter, it has been indicated that modern marketing practices
were implemented in French firms during the 1960s, which means at
least a decade or more after the USA. This has been explained by the
specific market context in France but also by the fact that in France,
some employees were reluctant to enter into a strong customer orientation within their firms: the marketing rhetoric adopted was really
just that, rhetoric associated with managerial edict, with no real intent
to operationalise marketing fully or seriously, *at that time*. This was
developed in the first section of the chapter. The second section of the
chapter used the case of Rodier, a French fashion brand company
which tried to develop a strong marketing concept but failed because
global customer satisfaction could not be reached and targeted customers who were attracted once did not come back again. There were
also mistakes associated with distribution ambience and the failure to
effectively forestall market inroads by competitive forces. This is,
therefore, an example of a French branded company that was unable

to make marketing rhetoric a form of reality experienced by customers in the marketplace. The last section of the chapter used the case of A-POC, a fashion brand launched by the fashion designer Issey Miyake who already had a strong brand image in France. As seen, this new launch proved a success because the firm was able to create a strong and real (or at least perceived by the customer as such) link between customers and the company, which satisfactorily served both the market and the company itself.

Some aspects of marketing, as witnessed previously, would indicate that France is still divided somewhat from most other developed industrialised nations. On the other hand, ethical issues associated with marketing rhetoric and practice are bringing the country (and its businesses) closer to the other industrialised nations in the world. Nonetheless, as seen in the Rodier example, sometimes the risks of premature death as a result of an inappropriate marketing relationship are run (Fournier, Dobscha and Mick, 1998). However, even if implementation of marketing within firms was not (and is not) always obvious, the marketing revolution is now part of France's economic and social reality. Information technologies will probably emphasise and exacerbate this trend in France (Bell *et al.*, 1997). Thus, in France, marketing is probably here to stay. Unfortunately for those businesses where marketing is practised as a form of rhetoric rather than reality, this spells a steadily decreasing market share. Customers will no longer take what is offered. Instead, non-delivery of promised satisfaction by businesses will result in the old adage being fulfilled: 'no customers, no business'.

The rhetoric and reality of marketing in the UK

3

martin evans

Aims

This chapter's aims are:

- to encourage reflection on the evolution and current operationalising of the marketing concept, in both marketing discourse and marketing practice
- to explore the 'reality' of 'the new marketing' in the context of contemporary claims of a new relationship paradigm
- to raise wider social responsibilities that marketing and marketers should take on board
- to position the first two aims within 'the new marketing' that is increasingly data-driven in order to be more accountable
- to explore the validity of the new relational marketing concept in an era of increasing consumer and marketer cynicism and whether at least some of this is mere rhetoric

Introduction

In the UK in recent years, many marketers have been witness to dramatic changes in their world. Markets have fragmented and technology provides for greater variation in production. Marketing itself can more easily identify more and smaller market segments, and it can target selected segments more effectively. In this respect, developments in the collection, analysis and use of personalised customer data have been major drivers of many of the developments in the 'new marketing' and, in this chapter, these issues are contextualised within how marketing itself is both conceptualised and operationalised.

Marketers' strategic objectives, for example, are often expressed in terms of the more recent paradigm shift to the relational vision. Practical attempts to operationalise this have had real implications for marketers and customers but these are not always positive. Developments over the last 20 years (especially) have meant that marketers are more able to analyse customer behaviour at an individual level, and they increasingly aim to be able to cultivate long-term relationships with those customers who contribute most to the financial position of the organisation. In this way, there has been much attention devoted to concepts such as relationship marketing, customer relationship management (CRM), and one-to-one marketing. It has to be said that much of this is rhetoric rather than reality, as will be discussed in this chapter, and the effects are to potentially damage much of marketing's fragile credibility.

The chapter is structured as follows. First, changes in the marketing concept are outlined, with particular focus on how data-driven marketing impacts the changing paradigm. The operational nature of data-driven relational marketing is briefly demonstrated and this leads to a critical analysis of how this might be leading us away from some of the fundamentals of the marketing concept. The wider impact of the new marketing upon society is briefly explored but the constraints of short-term accountability are proposed as being barriers to a full reinstatement of the marketing concept, never mind the societal marketing concept.

The marketing concept: evolution and UK application

Many commentators (e.g. King, 1965) saw the 1950s as the dawning of the marketing concept insofar as the UK was concerned. King plotted the well-rehearsed shift from a production orientation (between 1900 and 1930) to a sales orientation (between 1930 and 1950). The emerging marketing orientation of the 1950s was typified as being concerned with mutually satisfying exchanges between organisations and their customers. The paradigm shift was based on the importance of understanding customers and delivering desired satisfactions more effectively and efficiently than the competition.

This led to the much greater use of both quantitative and qualitative market research in order to understand customer behaviour and an explosion in the assimilation of a greater depth of conceptual underpinning, to explore and explain consumer behaviour from a behavioural science perspective. Research into the psychology of how consumers process information, how they respond to marketing activity, and many other similar issues led to greater understanding of branding and marketing communications practices.

The paradigm shift was from 'selling things' to 'helping customers buy benefits'. This might not always have been operationalised but the concept itself was generally applauded. Then along came 'data'.

The data-driven (alias relationship) marketing concept in the UK

The year 1981 was a watershed year for UK marketing and heralded a shift in both marketing practice and theory. The 1981 UK Census led to the first geodemographic system but was also major catalyst in providing alternatives to anonymised (traditional) market research samples of perhaps a thousand respondents, representing the entire population and profiled according to a few demographic descriptors. The new alternative was based on data from all households in terms of dozens of characteristics. The further fusion of geodemographics with personalised data from lifestyle surveys and from transactional data provides what marketers take to be a buying 'biography' of customers, and from this they think they can develop relationships with customers.

The 'new' approach claims to change the paradigm from a focus on one-off exchanges to one in which exchanges can be traced back to previous interactions and reflect an on-going process. This in turn can lead to increased satisfaction for the customer as well as facilitating brand loyalty and more accurate sales forecasting for the company.

The main operationalising of relationship marketing is via database marketing, because this provides the means to identify and track individual customers and their buying behaviour, calculate 'lifetime' value, and generate personalised marketing communications.

However, the more conceptual underpinning of relationship marketing involves trust, commitment mutual benefit, adaptation and regard for privacy (O'Malley and Tynan, 1999), although marketers are not overly concerned with inviting customers to establish mutual relationships. Consider the following advice to business:

> relationship marketing ... requires a two-way flow of information. This does not mean that the customer has to give you this information willingly, or even knowingly. You can use scanners to capture information, you can gather telephone numbers, conduct surveys, supply warranty cards, and use a data overlay from outside databases to combine factors about lifestyle, demographics, geographics, psychograhics, and customer purchases. (Schultz, Tannenbaum and Lauterborn, 1993)

This view, probably commonplace at that time, would define relationship marketing as an oxymoron.

Also, the supposed paradigm shift from focusing on one-off transactions is itself dubious. It is interesting to remember that even in the 1960s marketers were not concerned exclusively with one-off transactions. Retention strategies such as the old Green Shield Stamps example, and indeed the entire branding process, are clearly not concerned exclusively with acquisition. It is common sense that marketers want customers to return and spread goodwill about the product, brand or company.

Let me make two points here; first, the 'old' definitions of marketing often do include relational constructs: 'Marketing means customer orientation – a true alliance with the fellow at the other end of the pipeline, but it insists upon a course of action of mutual benefit' (Borch, 1957). Indeed, the relational concept that proposes past, present and future interaction between organisations and customers and wider 'networking' issues was suggested by Wroe Alderson in the 1950s: 'it means creating a pattern for dealing with customers or suppliers which persists because there are advantages in both sides' (Alderson, 1958). Also, the well-established 'adoption' construct within Diffusion-Adoption Theory is concerned with regular committed purchasing. So is relationship marketing really new and different?

The second point is the confusion over conceptualising relational approaches. In a recent talk on CRM the practitioner presenter (identity not disclosed, to save blushes) explored the issues involved and built up to a definition of CRM. This emerged as the management process that 'identifies, anticipates and satisfies customer requirements efficiently and profitably'! Hmmm; I seem to have heard this somewhere before.

One way of conceptualising the 'new' relational approach is to consider it analogous to human relationships, yet many studies are critical and conclude that the human relationship analogy is inappropriate (O'Malley and Tynan, 1999). 'Personalisation' in the form of sending relevant offers to named customers is not the same as developing and maintaining a true relationship. Perhaps the main 'difference' revolves around data-driven approaches in marketing.

The 'new marketing' metrics

For ease of illustration and integration, these 'metrics' are demonstrated via a typical sequence of application, in two hypothetical case studies.

Case I: new metrics for 'identikit acquisition strategies'

This case is based on a small mail-order wine business that is concerned about its customers and prides itself on providing more than just 'wine'. It also provides information about the types of wine and, their vineyard of origin as added values. In this way the company is marketing-oriented and tries to adopt the marketing concept in that it wants to be profitable but by satisfying customer requirements for more than just 'cheap wine'.

It is able to analyse current customer profiles in a variety of ways. For example, its transactional data can be analysed for Recency, Frequency and Monetary value (RFM) and Long Time Value (LTV). These are two important metrics in data-driven marketing and many software packages include algorithms for these metrics. With the RFM metric, the company identifies the 'recency, frequency and monetary value' of customers and those with the highest rating according to this measure could be selected for targeting, while those with poorer RFM scores might be ignored or even deselected. Just knowing that a customer has purchased from the organisation in the past is important but not sufficient. Marketers are clearly more interested in a customer who has purchased in the last six months than a customer who last bought from the organisation in 1997. Similarly a one-off purchase may also make a customer less attractive, so knowing how often they buy from the organisation is an important measure. The value of orders from the customer hardly requires further explanation, but the combination of these factors clearly could identify the better groups of customers to target. Another metric is the LVA (Lifetime Value Analysis). Lifetime is perhaps somewhat of an overstatement: it does not mean the lifetime of the customer, but rather a designated period of time during which they are a customer of your organisation. Depending on the type of products or services on offer, 'lifetime' might be as little as six months (as in purchases for baby products) or as long as 10 years (as in the automotive market).

Whatever period is relevant, however, the concept of what that customer is worth to the organisation in sales and profit terms over a period of time is a useful concept that can again inform target segment selection. The wine company went through this process and then profiled the post-codes of its 'best' customers. Four MOSAIC groups emerged as representing these best customers. MOSAIC is a geodemographics brand produced by Experian in UK (copyright Experian 2002) and which also exists in several European countries and USA. The four 'most likely' MOSAIC groups were found to be:

- 'Clever Capitalists'
- 'Chattering Classes'
- 'Ageing Professionals'
- 'Gentrified Villages'

The company clearly knows where these 'best' customers live because it has their addresses, but the next stage was to identify where, geographically, others within these four MOSAIC groups live. A map showing the 'hot spots' of where these groups are more likely to live (Figure 3.1) was produced by Experian and the company was then able to narrow its geographical coverage of UK to suit its own distribution operation. It wanted to focus rather more on the South-East region and so it then approached Experian for a list of names and addresses of prospects in that region who are in the selected four MOSAIC groups.

Experian was able to provide a mailing list and the company targeted these households in order to acquire more customers who, they hoped, via this 'identikit' approach, might also become 'best' customers in terms of RFM and LTV.

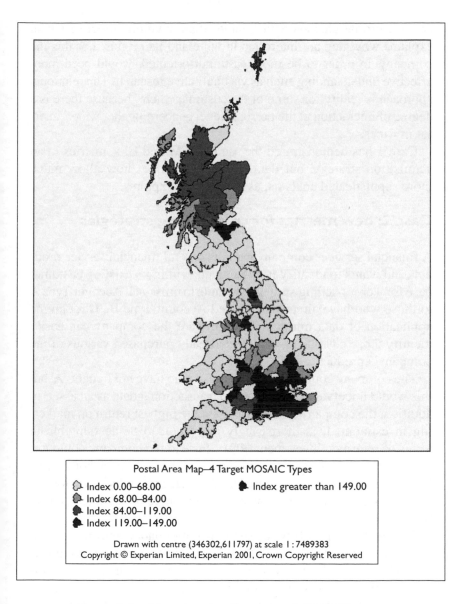

Postal Area Map—4 Target MOSAIC Types

⬥ Index 0.00–68.00   🌲 Index greater than 149.00
🌲 Index 68.00–84.00
🌲 Index 84.00–119.00
🌲 Index 119.00–149.00

Drawn with centre (346302,611797) at scale 1 : 7489383
Copyright © Experian Limited, Experian 2001, Crown Copyright Reserved

Figure 3.1   Map showing four target MOSAIC types

Even though the company is customer-oriented, the selection and targeting via this 'identikit' method of 'more of the same' does not, per se, lead to targeting those who really are interested in this form of added value in the wine market. These geodemographic characteristics are just profile characteristics, rather than anything affective which explains why they are interested in wine and its origins. For this the company, in order to be more customer-oriented, would need more affective understanding such as via qualitative research. The relational approach is reality for some of the customers here, because there is a degree of interaction at the personal level concerning the 'wider' interest in wines.

Case 1 has demonstrated the use of RFM and LTV metrics in an acquisition strategy, but data mining techniques now allow much more sophisticated analysis, as Case 2 now explores.

Case 2: new metrics for cross-selling strategies

A financial services company markets several financial service products and wants to identify new segments within its existing customer base for a cross-selling strategy. It wants to cross-sell Account Type A to those who have already purchased Account Type B. Through the application of data mining/CRM software the company can easily identify those customers who have already purchased various of the company's products.

The company could target all of these who have not bought 'A' but this would undervalue customer and transactional data as an asset. In addition, the company would also want the highest return on marketing investment. It is increasingly important to be accountable in terms of return on investment (ROI). Instead the company could use this software to interrogate existing customers who have both A and B accounts. Data mining can identify what makes these customers different from others and what makes them more or less likely to take both products.

The fullest benefit from existing customer data comes from looking at all of the attributes together. The easiest way to achieve this is via CHAID, which in this case is an integral component of the software being used and of most similar packages. In Figure 3.2, various customer and transactional attributes have been investigated to see which best explain what characterises customers who have both A and B. A 'tree' structure represents different 'hot' and 'cold' branches through the data. Each branch represents a different level of importance in explaining who the A and B customers are. Each attribute is assessed and the most important or 'significant' forms the first split. Taking the entire customer base in this instance, 26.44 per cent of all customers have both A and B accounts.

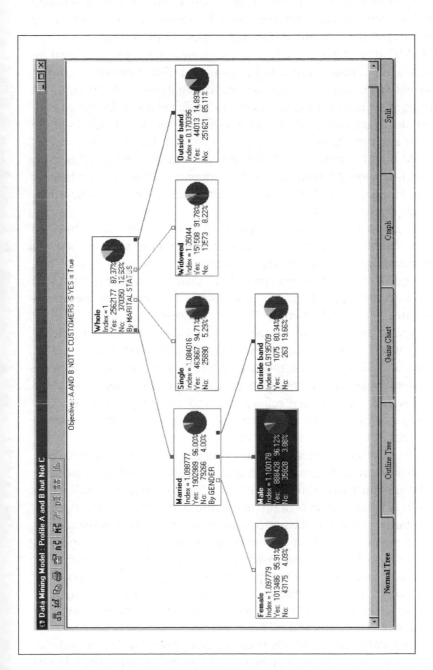

Figure 3.2 CHAID mining

By following the 'hottest branch' the company can understand which characteristics are possessed by those customers who have purchased both A and B Account types. Further branches of the CHAID tree might cascade down to even more segments based on whichever variables prove to be significant. Space prevents showing further stages here, but let us assume the analysis produced 60 target segments; each of these would have significant and different characteristics. Targeting could be done on a 'test' basis in which a sample from each might be targeted and those with better response rates could then be targeted with the full 'roll-out' campaign. Also, each could be targeted with different treatments, according to whatever gender, age, marital status or geodemographic characteristic might underpin the 'creative'.

There are claims with the approach described in this case study for 'relationship' marketing. Certainly the company is keen to maintain on-going interaction with its customers and encourage them to buy other products from the company. In this way it is certainly interested in more than one-off transactions, but is the reality of the operationalising of 'CRM' here really more rhetoric?

Again, there is focus on the metrics of data mining and little by way of real affective insight into customer needs. Historical transactions and identifying customer profiles are not good surrogates for implementing the marketing concept as it appears in discourse in the 1960s and 1970s or the relational paradigm from 1980s, and certainly not the societal marketing concept of the 1960s as explored earlier (and there will be more later).

The discussion so far, and a superficial analysis of the second case, probably gives the impression that we have moved to one-to-one relationship marketing, but this is very far from the truth. Dibb (2001) explores aspects of this and points out that 'at the heart of segmentation strategy is the notion that customers will allow themselves to be managed'. Indeed the use of the word 'management' in CRM might signal that 'relationship management' is an oxymoron. It implies power, and that that power is one-way. For customers to be 'locked in' to an air miles loyalty scheme, for example, might be music to the ears of the data-driven marketer, but do all customers appreciate being 'locked in'?

Such data analysis as has been outlined above can lead to individuals being targeted but not necessarily as individuals. The CHAID example demonstrated that although individual data was processed, the resulting segments are still aggregates even if their constituent members are targeted by name and address and probably with different styles of offer from those in other segments. Tesco, in the UK, has analysed its loyalty card data and it has been reported (Marsh, 2001) that by mining the mountain of transactional data from its 10 million Clubcard users, it has identified 100,000 different segments, each targeted with a different set of money-off vouchers via a customer magazine. A similar example is provided by Tower Records. This company has segmented its customer database and e-mails offers to selected targets, but 'out of every 10,000 e-mails sent, no more than three people receive the same offer' (Marsh, 2001).

The 'personalised' approach to relational marketing, however, might experience future flak. Digital printing technology, for example, allows personalisation to a higher degree: 'You can personalise page by page, it's easy to put a name anywhere throughout the copy' (Arnold, 2002). A development of this in USA was an apparently hand-written mailing targeted at members of a particular health care segment. So convincing was this that over 150 people complained on the basis that it looked like a friend writing to them telling them they needed to lose weight.

Technology will also facilitate more examples of personalised targeting of segments. It is possible to target an individualised television message, analogous to personalised mailing, to a unique address via fibre optic cable (Channel 4, 1990).

In practice, the most usual interpretation and operationalising of organisation–customer relationship is essentially this sort of data mining, which is used to identify and classify customer segments for differential targeting. It is unfortunate that many companies see a software package as all that is required. If the management of this resulting knowledge is not integrated and shared across relevant organisational functions, there is little chance of there being sustainable relational marketing. 'Knowledge management', as it is often termed, is a framework for moving data-driven marketing to a more strategic position. This is an approach that moves the narrower relationship marketing towards intra- and inter-company networks within the broader CRM paradigm.

More fundamentally, though, something more affective is needed. Needs and benefits sought by customers are not always considered to be as important as 'behaviour'. Some organisations are rejecting the more affective research in favour of purely behavioural data.

For example, the JIGSAW consortium, composed of Unilever, Kimberly-Clark and Cadbury Schweppes, has been pooling transactional data on their respective customers in order to grow product categories and to combat the power of intermediary retailers. This consortium has decided not to use attitudinal customer data any more and to base their marketing decisions on the massive amount of behavioural transactional data they (collectively) possess. Although this sort of alliance broadens and deepens the relational concept, in terms of 'networking' as mentioned above, it still lacks the fundamental constructs of even the 1950s marketing concept.

Gofton (2001) reports that the UK consultancy firm, Qci, found that few organisations distinguish between the satisfaction levels of their most and least valuable segments: 'Only 16% [of the 51 blue chip companies interviewed] understand what the main drivers of loyalty are … 30% never look at this and only half carry out some research to identify loyalty.' Indeed, a study amongst pharmaceutical companies found that when asked what the key challenges are for the introduction of CRM, only 6.5 per cent of the issues mentioned related to improving customer satisfaction (Clegg, 2001). The implications of the above, then, are that purely behavioural response does not necessarily equate with an understanding of consumers. Taking this further, if the 'behavioural' responders become the central focus then are we not we storing up trouble for the future in attending less to why the others are non-responders?

All in all, then, there are some concerns over the practicalities of relational marketing. It is surely the case that the data-driven approach will continue but will this lead to true organisation–customer relationships rather than just repeated exchange interactions? Even by 2001 there were signs that the bubble might have burst as Mitchell (2001b) reported that 'corporate disillusionment and downright hostility to the whole CRM bandwagon is reaching feverpitch'.

Perhaps marketers should be more honest; they want to track customer spending in order to target people with what would be hoped would be offers more likely to produce a purchase response. The problem with the 'R' word is that it has too many associations with human relationships but organisation–customer interaction is not the same, as discussed earlier. However, if it does fit at all, perhaps 'stalking' is the most relevant relational strategy? Indeed Brown (2000) even muses over whether RM refers in reality to 'Rip-Off Marketing'!

Another rather cynical note comes from research by Kennedy and Ehrenberg (2000) who suggest, with reference to 'brands', 'good old-fashioned mass marketing approaches to branding are what have made brands'. Could this be further support for revisiting earlier marketing theory?

Transactional and profiling data provides valuable information on who is buying what, when, how and where, but it is market research that can get beneath the surface even further and discover the 'why' of behaviour.

An interesting reinforcement of the problem raised here comes from a project funded by the UK Chartered Institute of Marketing (CIM) into the effects of technology on marketing and marketers (CIM, 2001). In this, marketers' commitment to understanding customers in the new era was explored and 'data' of the sort discussed above were often seen to be more important than qualitative understanding:

> I've been going to these groups for 20 years ... the number of occasions to which the director of marketing has turned up to these groups you can count on one hand ... therefore when a marketing director gets to present to the board, does he really know as much as the sales director sitting next to him? Very likely not. (Consultant, fast-moving consumer goods (FMCG) sector)

Mitchell (2001a) recently quoted a director of one of the largest retailers in UK:

> We've given up trying to understand our customers ... helping us cut a lot of complexity from our business. The academic's instinct is to gather a large amount of information, formulate a theory, and apply it to a situation ... [this] creates waste in the form of the wrong information at the wrong time, leading to the wrong decisions ... or ... fruitless attempts to predict or alter customer behaviour.

The favoured approach by this company, 'sense and respond' (Haeckel, 2001), is to react quickly on the basis of customer contact via call centres, the Internet, interactive digital television, and infomediaries. This is understandable in the current context of pressure to achieve short-term profit in order to provide shareholder value. However, it can lead to a subordination of the key components of the marketing concept itself, namely customer satisfaction and any customer understanding, other than what can be gleaned and inferred from, for example, tracking transactional data. Indeed, CRM has been manifested not in shared and managed customer knowledge across a learning organisation, but rather as the purchase of a software package.

Impact of the new marketing in the UK (and beyond)

Although the shift to data-driven marketing might mean that the focus of much customer understanding and strategic planning is narrower, by definition, it also brings with it wider social implications.

Data are, as has been discussed, increasingly 'personal'. This raises privacy issues. Take the first mentioned catalyst, the census. Names and addresses cannot be revealed from the census, but a link via the postal code system with the electoral roll means that it is possible to identify individual households and their characteristics. One of the current debates (at the time of writing) is between the Information Commissioner's position that the electoral roll was not collected for marketing purposes and should not therefore be used in this way, and on the other hand the marketing industry which argues for freedom in its use. Although the electoral roll is rarely used as a list in itself, it is used as the base for virtually every targeting tool, and geodemographics started this process. One concern of the Information Commissioner is that some people may disenfranchise themselves by not registering for fear of being overtargeted by marketers. A legal case has already brought this to a head. In November 2001 a member of the public won his case against Wakefield Council after that Council had not been able to confirm that his electoral roll data (name and address) would not be supplied to third parties without his consent, such as marketers (Acland, 2001). Having said this, it is likely that an opt-out clause will be added to the electoral roll and this should help to alleviate privacy concerns at the same time as shifting the marketing paradigm in yet another direction; 'permission marketing'. Perhaps customers will give permission to specific organisations to use their details for specified purposes.

The previously mentioned strategic alliance consortia approach between companies, in order to broaden the relationship concept and extend it beyond organisation–customer interaction to wider networks, has further social implications. If 'opt-out' boxes are not 'ticked', this will allow companies to use personal data 'within the group'. Do all customers know that 'the group' might not be merely 'the brand' they have just purchased (with which they might indeed like to have some sort of interactive exchange), but rather several multinational conglomerates (with whom they might not)?

The sharing of data has other implications. Mail Marketing, for example, is sharing some of its lists with Infocore, a US list company

(Wood, 1998). However, the 1997 European Data Protection Directive prevents all member countries from exporting personal information to countries that do not have adequate data protection and this includes the USA in the view of the EU. As the Information Commissioner has said, 'businesses exporting data must be satisfied that they comply with the law – otherwise I will simply prevent the activity' (France, 1998).

Another data source being used comes from the sky. In the UK an aerial photographic census is being created (Anonymous, 1999). Simmons Aerofilms and the National Remote Sensing Centre will be 'married with other data sets such as Census information and demographic details' (Stannard, 1999). Some people might see this as an uncontrollable invasion of privacy.

The possible acquisition of genetic data is another potential concern (Specter, 1999) and perhaps even more serious ethical issues are likely to need addressing here. The accessing of individual medical records might be considered to be an invasion of privacy if what is thought to be confidential between doctor and patient is shared across financial services companies. In a survey of 3,000 UK households, three-quarters were against genetic tests for insurance underwriting, 85 per cent against insurance companies rejecting applicants on this basis and 78 per cent against insurance companies charging higher premiums on the basis of genetic tests. Indeed, 68 per cent of the sample thought that this use of genetic data should be prohibited by law (Borna and Avila, 1999). Introna and Powlouda (1999) report that medics have expressed concern over this trend. The logical extension of the scenario is that those who do not need insuring will be insured and the rest will be excluded.

Another consideration is that data fusion itself has been assessed as 'not containing much in the way of internal validity checks, creating the real possibility that decisions will be made using a fused database which does not represent reality' (Jephcott and Bock, 1998). So all of the above might lead to a kind of 'future shock' if the resulting targeting is based upon flawed analysis.

A further area of relevance to any wider social responsibility of (data-driven) marketing is the purchase of marketing data by government departments. CACI, for example, have an entire department dealing exclusively with government contracts for ACORN and related products. Geodemographic systems use an increasing range of financial data sources to overlay census, housing and demographic data, and the resulting 'financial' ACORN and MOSAIC products can easily be seen to be of potential value to the Inland Revenue (for example) to check financial details and trends against tax returns from those they want to investigate further. The UK Inland Revenue is also able to access individualised transaction data from supermarket loyalty schemes for those cases of potential tax fraud that it investigates (Key, 2000). Claimed levels of poverty on the tax return can be compared with actual purchase behaviour. Would consumers be so willing to sign up for these schemes if this was known?

The UK government has been interested in loyalty scheme data for another purpose. The idea was to track consumers' food consumption patterns with a view to assessing the impact of genetically modified foods (Hansard, 1999; Parker, 1999).

Is this the point beyond which the use of personal data, supposedly for marketing, becomes unacceptable? Or is it entirely justified to use such data to investigate a serious health issue of public concern?

The LTV and RFM analysis (discussed earlier) can lead to those customers who are not considered to be strong contributors to the company being deselected. They would not be sent relevant offers or, in the case of financial services, for example, they would be offered accounts which require higher initial deposits than they can afford. Indeed the Halifax bank was discovered, via a flip chart left in a hotel room after a company training session, to refuse to allow certain groups of people, to be customers at all (Mackintosh, 2002).

There are signs that the problem has been recognised by government; it has set up a social exclusion department and is concerned about banks closing branches in favour of direct approaches because of potential exclusion effects within some sections of the community. In the USA the Community Reinvestment Act is supposed to prevent banks from closing in poor neighbourhoods, so perhaps there are signs of the tide turning with respect to these sorts of wider social responsibility issues, but at a political rather than at a marketing level. There are doubts about the likely outcome, though. Political lobbying by companies via public relations and the 'political donation' system, to influence competition and other legislation in companies' favour, is often more powerful and decisive.

In general terms, though, the preceding analysis points to confused and inconsistent interpretations of the marketing concept. Brown (1999) suggests that the 'proponents of marketing orientation have become product oriented'. Perhaps much operationalising of marketing has regressed to the selling concept. Boyter (2002) points to conflicts amongst marketers. He discusses a 'barrier' to marketing being driven by what is known about customers in terms of a 'conflict between sales force-driven and data driven marketing ... [Some] companies still just need to feed their sales force.' Does this suggest that there are those who are data driven (bringing the issues discussed in this chapter) and those who are still operating at a sales concept level?

So, is it time to revisit marketing theory as it was proposed 30 years ago? It might not have always lived up to its ideals when operationalised, but at least the ideals were not pretentious, unachievable, confused or inconsistent.

Maybe it is time to reconsider the societal marketing concept?

Indeed the analysis does not just lead us back to the earlier marketing concept but to one in which a wider role for marketing was included. As Lazer (1969) suggested: 'Marketing must serve not only business but also the goals of society ... its responsibilities extend well beyond making profits ... and its contributions extend well beyond the formal boundaries of the firm.' Lavidge (1970) also criticised marketing's failure to help to deal with social rather than economic problems. Indeed, more recently, Cova (1999) suggested that because economic activity is inevitably embedded within a societal context, marketing 'can be defined less as the launching of a product on a market than as the ascribing of a meaning in a society'. Indeed, he explores yet another potential paradigm shift: from marketing to societing.

The recent relational concept has also attracted criticism, as this chapter has mentioned. Customers are also not always convinced by it either, as reported by Evans, O'Malley and Patterson (2001). Consumer quotes, such as the following, reflect this:

■ 'I don't mind companies knowing more about me but that bit about meeting your needs is a load of bullshit'
■ 'They target what they think you are interested in'

That research concluded that many consumers are 'cynical and critical of marketing activity which they consider to be frivolous, insulting, intrusive and/or generally inappropriate' (Evans, O'Malley and Patterson, 2001).

The above discussion of how marketers are using data (and perhaps verging on abusing it, in some cases) suggests a reciprocal cynicism on the part of some marketers. Consider marketers' reactions to issues that have been suggested in this chapter as being not only important, but which might even offer relational opportunities if they are addressed positively. The following are headlines in the UK trade magazine, *Precision Marketing*, between November 2001 and February 2002:

- 'Uproar across industry as decision favours privacy' (*Precision Marketing*, December 2001)

- 'DMA poised to fight electoral roll ruling' (*Precision Marketing*, December 2001)

- 'Industry bodies slam new SMS Preference Service' (*Precision Marketing*, January 2002)

- 'Net industry in Uproar as EU plans to abolish Cookies' (*Precision Marketing*, November 2001)

So, on the one hand, there are arguments for wider social responsibilities of marketing to be taken on board, while on the other hand there are increasing pragmatic pressures for marketers to narrow their focus to short-term profits and shareholders, and perhaps for them rather cynically to reject social concerns. The latter probably makes the former an idealistic pipe-dream made in cloud-cuckoo land.

The new UK marketer

There are, however, some final implications for marketers themselves. Underpinning at least some of the above is a possible 'skills gap'. The CIM research into the effects of technology on marketing and marketers (CIM, 2001) brings disquieting news:

> Marketers should develop IT [information technology]/new technology skills – (maybe via 'junior mentors' – younger people who are 'IT savvy' and who can educate their senior colleagues). We cannot influence the development and usage of IT within companies unless we know something about it. (Senior manager, financial services multinational, as cited by CIM, 2001)

Indeed, Carson (1999) interviewed a group of leading US marketing practitioners and concluded that analytical skills and statistics topped the list of 'areas in which their education was lacking'.

The CIM (2001) study reinforces this and shows that businesses are demanding more accountability than ever before, making it essential for marketers to be able to deal with the following.

1 'Know how to do the numbers and prove their financial contribution to the bottom line.' (Senior manager, financial services multinational)

2 'Before you address the skills we need to address more basic problems: do marketing people understand money? Cash flow? ROI? These are rhetorical questions to which the answer is "no".'

3 'How many times have marketers actually got outside their comfort zone and really got their hands dirty with this new technology? Unless you know how difficult it actually is, it's easy to under-estimate the time and effort in getting these things off the ground. I know because I've been a one-man band for the last ten years, but most marketers just hand over a brief to IT. And then when IT turn round and say no, marketers don't know enough to challenge it.' (Consultant, strategic branding)

The CIM (2001) report is important and marketing academics themselves should also take this on board because it has implications for their own course design and delivery. As marketing is increasingly driven by marketing databases and strives to achieve a degree of personalised and interactive customer (relationship?) management, marketing students would benefit from being able to deal with customer modelling and database analysis. Already we are seeing non-marketers taking over some of this ground and marketers losing, for example, control of websites as reported by the CIM (October 2000). Might this add to the sort of reversal of the marketing concept suggested in this chapter?

Summary and conclusions

In conclusion, the submission here is that data-driven marketing in UK is 'taking over' and facilitating greater (short-term) accountability via the more effective identification of those segments likely to be more profitable. Data lead to targeting those who are known to buy in that product category on the basis of data fusion and their resulting biographics.

The new marketing is becoming increasingly reliant upon the metrics of RFM, LTVs, CHAID and data mining. The danger is that these are subverting the role and importance of more affective research that aims to explain why customers behave as they do, rather than just whether and how they behave. The subversion is undermining the marketing concept itself and the rhetoric of the relationship marketing oxymoron is in danger of reducing the credibility of marketing and marketers. Marketers are seen to be increasingly cynical by increasingly cynical consumers.

It is interesting to go back in time one more time and remember a prediction from Shubik (1967): 'the computer and modern data processing provide the refinement – the means to treat individuals as individuals rather than parts of a large aggregate … the treatment of an individual as an individual will not be an unmixed blessing. Problems concerning the protection of privacy will be large.' This is not a misprint; it was 1967. However, as appears to be the case with customer deselection and social exclusion legislation, marketing will not make the change (after all, marketers will be thinking of the security of their own jobs); this would have to come from political change forced by a societal backlash. But is this likely? Political lobbying by companies in the UK (and indeed non-UK companies lobbying the UK government) not only to maintain the status quo but even to influence changes in legislation in ways favourable to themselves, plus the increasing use by political parties themselves of data-driven approaches, are likely to outweigh any social pressure.

Thus, the position of this chapter is that marketing activities are increasingly being pressed to be more accountable and cost effective, perhaps at the expense of achieving the ideals of the marketing concept. Could it be that the latter, whether the 'customer satisfaction' version of the 1960s and 1970s or the 'relational' version from the 1980s, are really too idealistic to operationalise in today's competitive environment? The 'Societal Marketing Concept' is perhaps even more idealistic. The result is plenty of rhetoric concerning customer focus and relationships, but is the reality that companies are really just trying to get more money from their customers? Certainly they will not achieve this by continuously producing poor products at extortionate prices, so a degree of customer satisfaction is clearly part of the reality, but it could be argued that the main focus is on (continuous) sales, in which case are we seeing yet another emerging concept: the *sustainable sales concept*? Or is this proposition itself rhetoric rather than reality?

Questions

1 What is 'marketing'? What, ideally, should it be? What, pragmatically, can it be?

2 To what extent can 'data-driven' marketing satisfy the philosophical constructs of the marketing concept and achieve anything approaching 'relational' interaction with customers?

3 Do marketers of the future need new skills? If so, what and why; if not, why not?

4 To what extent should marketing and marketers be concerned with the impact they have beyond immediate campaigns, or even outside longer-term brand and relational strategies?

5 Is *rhetoric* THE *reality* of the relational paradigm? Is *reality* based around long-term sales?

The rhetoric and reality of marketing in Cyprus

4

ioanna papasolomou-doukakis

Aims

This chapter presents research carried out within the Cypriot retail-banking sector regarding the ways that internal marketing helped change the culture of the sector to become more customer focused. We start by reviewing just what internal marketing is, adding our own interpretation of this marketing initiative. After a short presentation of the research methods, four core themes are explored which constitute internal marketing, namely:

- internal customers
- training and education
- quality standards
- reward systems

The findings indicate a marked difference between what marketing rhetoric promises versus what is actually delivered (i.e., the reality) in the two organisations that participated in the study.

What is internal marketing?

The Cypriot retail banking industry is a competitive business. There is increased pressure on retail banks in Cyprus to improve their services in order to differentiate themselves from the competition both within the country and also in view of the island's EU entry in 2004. It is the relative homogeneity and tough competition within the industry that led banks towards implementing service quality programmes as a means of attempting to gain competitive advantage. Varey and Lewis (1999) suggested that service orientation had become a key source of competitive advantage, a position also supported by Kasper, Helsdingen and Vries (1999) who insist that only a 'service attitude' among staff can lead to the delivery of outstanding customer service and help to increase market, mind and heart share. In this scenario, where does internal marketing fit?

Internal marketing is a managerial initiative which views internal relationships and structures within the organisation as governed by the same exchange logic that (apparently) presides over external markets. Consequently, if the organisation implements effective exchanges between its members, its departments, and between the organisation and various groups of employees, this will eventually underpin successful exchanges between the organisation and its customers. Gronroos (2000) argues strongly that without well-functioning *internal* relationships, external relationships will not develop successfully. Internal marketing focuses on the creation of effective internal relationships between people at all levels in the organisation via the development of service and customer-oriented individual mindsets. It is in this sense that internal marketing can act as a culture change programme agent which aims to transform the organisation along the lines of service quality and customer drive. While the rhetoric of internal marketing seems all-embracing, in reality, companies tend to focus merely on those employees actually involved in service encounters – the front-line or contact staff – with a view to ensuring that they improve their performance in terms of customer interaction. Support and technical staff may be left out and this could create a 'them and us' culture, which often hinders smooth organisational functioning.

In the banks considered in this study, it was the recognition of the important role that *all* employees can play in achieving customer satisfaction which led to the adoption of internal marketing. In the words of one bank manager: 'the nature of the job has changed ... we have to develop people for specific roles because the bank's role has changed significantly in the last ten years ... branch personnel need to become more customer focused and service oriented. Internal marketing is intended to achieve that.'

Through a number of rituals, banks in Cyprus have attempted to affect the way in which employees behaved with respect to each other, the organisation, and (more importantly) with respect to their external customers. As mentioned, four rituals appeared to be at the core of the internal marketing initiative, namely:

- internal customers
- training and education
- internal service standards
- reward strategies

Implicit in these four rituals, internal marketing programmes present in these retail banks all have a strong human resource management (HRM) flavour and apparently constitute an integral part of service quality initiatives. Internal marketing aims to attend to the needs of both internal and external customers. Typically, this is achieved through HRM levers that aim to inculcate a service mentality and reward those who are quick to internalise these new values. The evidence suggests that this process of value inculcation and culture change is not straightforward and unproblematic but one fraught with difficulties, conflict and ambiguity.

The banking industry in Cyprus

The last four decades have marked the transformation of the Cyprus Republic from a backward and poor agricultural society to one that is modern and flourishing. The accession of Cyprus to the EU will accelerate its role in international cooperation, as the country is uniquely poised to serve as Europe's outpost and bridge to the Middle East and beyond. Cyprus has the potential to grow into a major world economic centre. Its geographical position at the meeting point of three continents – Europe, Asia and Africa – and its already well-developed infrastructure provide the foundation for further economic growth. The island's accession to the EU is desirable in order to bring new challenges and opportunities, increase capital flows, accelerate technological advancement, and inculculate managerial know-how. However, it requires early restructuring and other adjustments in various sectors of the economy in order to set the country in the way of steady progress. The banking sector in particular has over the last few years experienced aggressive competition and turbulence not only from constituent banks, but also from cooperative societies. As a result, banks have focused their efforts on the following:

- providing high quality customer service through competitive products and specialised services
- increasing productivity and profitability by investing in technology
- enriching the range of services and products offered through private banking services
- strengthening profitability and efficiency ratios (Triantafyllides, 1999)

An integral part of the accession process is the liberalisation of interest rates and the abolition of the ceiling for the lending rate of interest, which is determined by law, and the free movement of capital. The island's accession to the EU suggests that Cyprus will soon abide by the laws and provisions of the EU, which allows for free movement of capital, and determination of the interest rates in a free market. The banking sector will change further as a result of the full liberalisation of the interest rate regime and the islanders' borrowing from abroad. Local banks will compete against each other in the setting of interest rates, and also with foreign banks in the granting of loans to Cypriots in foreign currency. Other measures that have to be introduced in order to modernise the sector include privatisation, the limitation of state controls, further liberalisation of foreign investments so that foreign funds are attracted into Cyprus, and cooperation between local businesses and indigenous and foreign corporations (Triantafyllides, 1999).

According to Triantafyllides (1999), the Cypriot banking sector will also be influenced by the following developments:

- various trends in the international financial services sector (e.g., mergers and acquisitions, and the evolution of Internet banking and telephone banking)
- developments in the Cypriot economy emerging from the harmonisation/liberalisation procedures
- the role of Cyprus as a regional financial centre and the need to provide services to current and potential services as they expand to new markets such as the Balkans or the Middle East

The increasingly competitive climate of the Cypriot banking sector prompted Cypriot banks to emphasise even more the importance of sales as a driving force. Banks undertook aggressive selling efforts to stimulate demand in order to absorb excess supply. Effort focused on activities such as cross-selling, and an aggressive pushing of products and services. The role of marketing management and entire marketing departments diminished to that of salespeople and sales support. Indeed 'marketing' is interpreted as primarily selling. Perhaps of necessity, Cyprus banks have misconstrued the underlying principles and implications of the marketing concept, mistakenly believing that it is all to do with finding ways to develop strong convictions among target customers about their brands with the short-term perspective of turning bank products into cash (preferably at the earliest opportunity). Banks have failed to appreciate that there is a need for a fundamental evaluation and understanding of their customers' needs and to discover the best ways of serving them. Banks have created and nourished a seller's market, wherein banks have been selling their products with little or no marketing effort to their target customers.

However, the future may well be different, as the banking system has an extremely important role to play in the national economy and, hence, it has to follow international standards and developments. Presumably marketing will have an important role to play?

The relationship between internal and external marketing: the theory

The marketing concept is taken to be managerial commitment to 'satisfying the needs and wants of target customers', to which Kotler (2000) adds, 'more effectively and efficiently than the competition'. Piercy and Morgan (1990) and Palmer (1994) stipulate that marketing should not be confined to the external market of customers but, instead, it must be practised internally within the organisation in order to make external marketing strategies work. Caruana and Calleya (1998) and R.C. Lewis (1989) claim that an organisation needs to be involved in external *and* internal marketing in order to achieve successful marketing. The key rationale is that the prime objective of internal marketing is the creation of an internal environment in which customer consciousness becomes an organisational imperative.

The core aim of traditional marketing is to match the organisational needs and wants to those of the environment within which it operates. Internally, the marketing function is responsible for the promotion and selling of customer-orientation throughout the organisation (Kotler and Andreasen, 1991). In doing that it deals with internal and external markets where success in the latter is dependent on success in the former (Flipo, 1986). The interdependence of the internal and external strategies is illustrated by a triangular, bipolar set of relations, as shown in Figure 4.1.

The core objective of internal marketing is to create motivated and customer-conscious personnel at every level (Cowell, 1984; George, 1990; George and Gronroos, 1989; Gronroos, 1981a,b) in order to

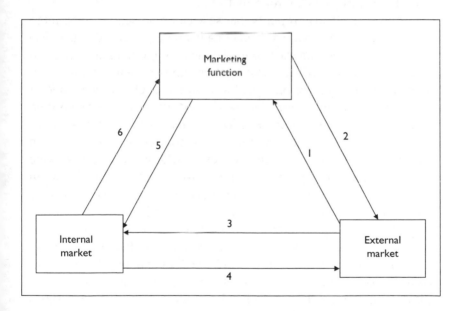

The first pole is the external market: its behaviour influences that of contact personnel (4) and the strategy defined by the marketing manager (1). The second pole is the internal market: its behaviour influences that of customers (3) and the internal strategy defined by the marketing manager (6). The third pole is the marketing function: its strategy influences the behaviours both of the external (2) and the internal (5) markets. (Flipo, 1986, p. 7)

Figure 4.1   The inter-relationship between internal and external markets
Source: Adapted from Flipo (1986), p.7.

meet the needs of external customers. George (1990) and Gronroos (1981b; 1984b) stipulate that the internal market of employees is best motivated for service-mindedness and customer-oriented behaviour by an active and marketing-like approach where different activities are used internally in a marketing-oriented way. The underlying assumption of internal marketing is that personnel are the first market of a company (Berry, 1981). B.R. Lewis (1991), Judd (1987), Band (1991) and Ciampa (1992) claim that the internal exchanges between the organisation and its employee groups must be operating effectively before the organisation can be successful in achieving its goals in the external markets. Hence, internal marketing becomes a prerequisite for successful external marketing performance (Compton *et al.*, 1987; Gronroos 1985).

Gronroos (1984a) proposes that service organisations need more than just traditional external marketing in order to succeed in the marketplace: they need interactive marketing and internal marketing. All three types of marketing, whose relationship is known as the *services marketing triangle*, are presented in Figure 4.2. On the right side of the triangle are the *external marketing* efforts that the organisation undertakes in order to prepare, price, distribute and promote services to customers. Across the bottom of the triangle is what has been termed *interactive marketing*, which is where the actual service delivery takes place: there is face-to-face interaction between employees and customers. The left side of the triangle stipulates the vital role played by *internal marketing*, which is aimed at enabling employees to keep the promises made to customers (Kotler, 1997).

Internal marketing is based on the assumption that employee and customer satisfaction are closely linked (Zeithaml and Bitner, 1996) with the former being a prerequisite for the latter (Fisk, Brown and Bitner, 1993; Pfau, Detzel and Geller, 1991). Heskett *et al.* (1994) stipulate that successful service organisations concentrate their focus on both the customers and employees. The service–profit chain that links a service organisation's profits with employee and customer satisfaction consists of five links, which illustrate the close relationship between employee and customer satisfaction (Heskett *et al.*, 1994):

■ healthy service profits and growth – superior service from performance, which results from ...

■ satisfied and loyal customers – satisfied customers who remain loyal, repeat purchase, and refer other customers, which results from ...

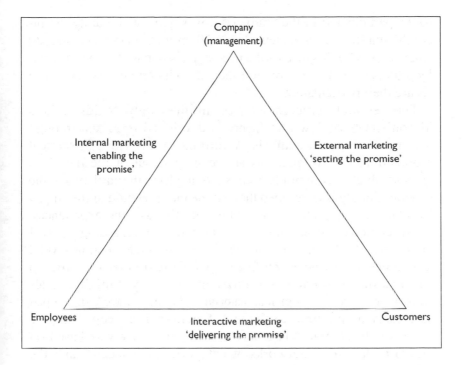

Figure 4.2   The services marketing triangle
Source: Adapted from Gronroos (1984), p.24.

- greater service value – more effective and efficient customer value creation and service delivery, which results from ...
- satisfied and productive service employees – more satisfied, loyal and hard-working employees, which results from ...
- internal service quality – superior employee selection and training, a quality work environment, and strong support for those dealing with customers

Case research method

The study was qualitative in nature since its main aim was to uncover people's views and experiences rather than reflect objectively an a priori reality. An initial study was done with UK banks and then applied to Cyprus. The findings from the UK and Cyprus were entirely different. In Cyprus, 30 business units from two different banks participated in the study. Data was generated mainly via in-depth qualitative interviews with 20 branch managers and 20 employees. The disguise of the two banks is due to the confidentiality promised by the researcher to the research participants in order to secure their participation.

The research process adopted in the study builds around Mason's (1996) view that theory is developed from and through data generation and analysis. According to this view, theoretical propositions or explanations are developed out of the data in a process which is commonly seen as moving from the particular to the general. Theory is developed through the interpretation of the empirical data, and is grounded in reality (in this case, the experiences, interpretations and actions of the interviewees regarding internal marketing). Data analysis was carried out by implementing several techniques as instructed by Strauss and Corbin (1990) in order to enhance the *theoretical sensitivity* of the study. Initially, codes were attached to the empirical material and concepts were developed as closely as possible to the text. Later, such concepts become increasingly abstract. The development of theory was based on the formulation of networks of categories or concepts and the relationships between them.

Four major rituals appear to constitute internal marketing in the banks studied: the image of the internal customer; training and education; quality standards; and rewards systems. By pursuing these four initiatives concomitantly, Cypriot retail banks aim to create a culture where service-mindedness and customer-orientation become central values.

It is the view of banks' management that the image of the '*internal customers*' helps in terms of fostering a service mentality by encouraging individual employees to focus on delivering high service quality in their internal service encounters. By making the image of 'internal customers' central to the way in which employees perceive themselves and one another, managers aim to achieve internal customer satisfaction as a prerequisite for external customer satisfaction. A branch manager said: 'If everyone accepts that they have internal customers to serve then their attitudes and their behaviour towards each other will improve because you want to treat everybody in a way that you would like to be treated. This will then reflect on the way we treat our external customers.' Gummesson (2000) suggests that it has become established in the quality management literature that employees are internal customers and that the ability of an employee to satisfy the needs of others inside the organisation is a precondition for external customer satisfaction.

The banks studied rely heavily on *development programmes* that teach employees how to be customer-focused and service-orientated. These programmes, entitled either customer care or customer service programmes, aim to instil a customer/service ethos within branch networks. In particular, these courses aim to help staff understand the importance of striving to meet the internal service standards in their internal interactions as a prerequisite for achieving external customer satisfaction. The overarching aim is to develop a strong service mentality that will pervade the entire organisation. Banks make use of training and education programmes in order to promote the view that employees' attitudes and behaviours towards customers form an integral part of the overall service offering. Developmental programmes reinforce the internal customer concept with a view to improving staff competencies and ultimately customer service. These developmental programmes help individuals to identify their internal customers and understand their needs and wants (Pfau, Detzel and Geller, 1991) thus contributing to the realisation of successful internal encounters and satisfied external customers (Lewis and Entwistle, 1990). A branch manager stated:

> Internal marketing [IM] has changed the nature of training. Now it's more about being customer focused and service oriented. IM helps employees give more professional service. A lot of the training programmes are aimed at highlighting the importance of achieving service quality in the internal encounters and treating your fellow workers as internal customers. As a result customer and service orientation are strengthened.

Internal performance standards are another ritual that forms an integral part of the internal marketing initiative. In the banks studied, internal standards are designed by head offices along the lines of service quality, behaviour and integrity. The rationale behind them is that branch managers and employees will see these standards as vital in managing and achieving internal service quality and service delivery quality. To check compliance with these standards, formal performance assessment and monitoring procedures are carried out within each branch. Written reports are produced and communicated by the head office to all concerned branches *vis-à-vis* the performance achieved by the individuals and the business unit as a whole.

Fourth, the reward systems in place within these banks appear to be correlated with customer service targets. The intrinsic and extrinsic rewards for performance achieved in terms of service quality and customer focus are among the core elements of the internal marketing practice. Banks primarily link the achievement of service quality with:

- monetary awards
- non-monetary rewards such as gifts, medals, plaques and travel coupons
- intrinsic rewards, such as service awards presentation ceremonies and public praise

Despite the overall sentiment expressed in these aggregate findings, let us now turn to the examples of marketing 'reality', and then marketing 'rhetoric'.

Case 1: Alpha bank: taking care of those who take care of customers!

The metaphor of the 'internal customer' lies at the centre of internal marketing initiatives. By ostensibly giving the employees the status of internal customers, top management aims to affect the exchanges between them in such a way that they become more motivated to perform their duties towards the next person in the value chain more effectively. Analysis of employees' perceptions reveals that employees expect to be treated in a caring way by their superiors and feel valued by the organisation. Analysis of managers' views shows that the successful implementation of internal marketing via the effective use of the internal customer imagery may aid managers in their efforts to demonstrate a caring attitude towards their subordinates, and this in turn will motivate employees to exhibit positive attitudes towards external customers. In the enthusiastic verbiage of a branch manager:

> if the internal marketing ideas are successfully implemented then managers won't have to persuade their subordinates to develop positive attitudes towards the external customers. Because the internal marketing ideas suggest that in order to take care of your customers, you must first take care of those who take care of the customers, hence your employees. Happy and satisfied employees create happy and satisfied customers. Employee feelings of satisfaction will reflect on the level of service delivered to internal and external customers.

It is management's belief that internalisation of the internal customer role creates an *internal service mentality* that is conducive to delivering *external* high-quality customer service. Emphasising the importance of each individual in achieving service quality in every internal customer/supplier interaction is a prerequisite for enabling personnel to deliver high-quality customer service. The notion that everybody has 'internal customers' to serve may help staff understand that everybody's effort affects the level of service delivered to external customers, and that successful service provision is dependent on interpersonal exchanges between all service personnel. In management's view, customer satisfaction and retention is achieved when every individual accepts the idea that service quality is everybody's concern. A fast-track employee said, for example:

> IM emphasises the importance of providing service quality to your internal customers. Only then the organisation will be able to achieve high quality customer service ... it instils a service mentality throughout the organisation by emphasising the notion of treating employees as internal customers ... it highlights the importance of meeting the internal service standards as a prerequisite for achieving internal customer satisfaction. High quality internal service creates high quality customer service and hence, satisfaction.

According to the managers interviewed, banks are in a better position to satisfy their external customers by first designing internal products that satisfy the needs of the internal customers. At the heart of the internal marketing initiatives within this organisation is the view that the needs of internal customers must first be fulfilled, prior to (and as a prerequisite for) satisfying the needs of external customers. To do so, most of the banks contained within the Alpha Group have embarked on internal market research in an attempt to identify, assess and measure internal customer expectations in terms of, for example, internal customers' needs and concerns, internal service quality levels and internal service quality gaps. One of the branch managers said: 'we have done internal surveys to investigate subordinates' views regarding their superiors on issues such as motivation, training opportunities, expressing ideas.' Selling the bank's products to employees is another way in which employees are being transformed into internal customers. This is an activity typically implemented by head offices. Its purpose is the enhancement of the employees' knowledge and competences in relation to the bank's products. Banks encourage their personnel to purchase the bank's products in order to generate (1) custom; and (2) more in-depth knowledge of products to share with other customers.

The Alpha Group has implemented a number of *training and development programmes* that emphasise customer focus and service orientation. Most aim to inculcate a service mentality throughout the organisation by emphasising the importance of treating employees as internal customers. In the internal marketing context, training is mainly directed at 'shaping' employees' attitudes and behaviour towards recognising the importance of both internal and external customers and acting to meet their demands. An employee suggested:

> If you can portray an attitude of caring and helping individuals to improve not only for their ability to do the job but also for their personal satisfaction, you'll get far more positive attitudes. IM emphasises the importance of being customer focused all the time. Many of the training courses are aimed at changing staff attitudes towards their colleagues and customers.

This banking organisation aims to instil confidence that the extra energy which individuals voluntarily invest will be reflected in their performance appraisals and their *rewards*. The intrinsic and extrinsic rewards for performance achieved in terms of service quality and customer focus are among the core elements of internal marketing practice. The organisation primarily links the achievement of service quality with: (1) intrinsic rewards such as service awards presentation ceremonies and public praise; (2) non-monetary rewards such as gifts, and travel coupons; and (3) the use of monetary rewards based on the performance achieved by teams, not individuals. An employee said: 'Being rewarded and praised for our efforts to provide exceptional service is a key performance motivator. IM emphasises the importance of recognising and rewarding good performance in terms of service quality both internal and external.'

Such incentives aim to ensure that the relationship between the organisation and individual employees is optimised; but, in exchange, individual employees are expected to treat their colleagues as customers and deliver a high standard of service, as they themselves would expect in the external marketplace. According to a branch manager:

> If you treat people the way you want to be treated, the quality of internal service will improve. Everybody needs to be given the same standard of service. The notion of internal customers highlights that. Internal Marketing encourages everybody to provide each customer, internal and external, with the best possible service.

The message of the importance of internal customer appeared to have been internalised by some employees, one of whom said:

> If people share the idea that they all have internal customers to serve, which is at the 'heart' of Internal Marketing, they will be motivated to provide good internal service. If you provide good internal service then you would expect others to provide good service ... the bank actually went through a phase of defining the different departments as internal customers. The internal customer idea makes people more aware [that it is] not only the front line personnel who deliver service to the customer ... everybody is part of the service chain.

The effective implementation of internal marketing has the potential to improve employee attitudes and the quality of the internal service interactions by demonstrating a 'people-oriented mentality'. This organisation appears to have realised that customer satisfaction starts from within. Excellent service contributes to achieving external customer satisfaction:

> The key idea of IM is recognising and demonstrating that people are important which is necessary in a service organisation ... more and more staff are feeling valued ... this motivation is something we've got to look to as the industry becomes more competitive. If we see that the organisation treats us as individuals, cares for our development, we will feel valued. If we are happy then we will work better together and this will reflect on the service we provide to our customers. (from an interview with an employee)

A branch manager said:

> I consider IM a key factor in creating a motivating environment. It's vital to our organisation because it enables us to portray a caring attitude to our people. If employees are happy and satisfied then the chances are that they will stay, perform well, and feel part of the same team.

In essence, the staff in this organisation perceive an improvement in the customer focus and service orientation of the organisation, a key element in achieving a marketing orientation. Overall, this study demonstrates that internal marketing affects both how the individual interprets their role within the organisation, and how these roles relate to the wider operation of the organisation. However, like any initiative designed to alter the culture of an organisation, it cannot succeed without purposive coordination, assessment and control.

With some reservations, in this bank, the adoption of internal marketing appears to extend beyond rhetoric to a form of marketing that is perceived positively by the central group, the branches, and by management and personnel in the branches themselves. At this broad macro level, Alpha Group appear to have achieved 'marketing reality'. Of course, an assessment of how successful the IM campaign has been in improving external customer service, quality perceptions, brand loyalty and new custom has not yet been carried out and it needs to be. If, for example, an IM initiative is successful, and yet does not produce any appreciable benefits with 'real customers', then the whole ethos of IM will need to be re-evaluated. Let us now turn to the second case example.

Case 2: Omega Bank: taking care of those who take care of customers? Not really!

Despite the recognition of the importance of viewing and treating employees as internal customers, the increasingly hostile and unpredictable competitive environment of the Cypriot financial services industry has forced this bank to change the role and structure of the branch network, resulting in significant reductions in terms of branch outlets and staff numbers. Some staff members have been forced to take involuntary redundancy with the concomitant effect of employee uncertainty and lowered staff morale for those left behind. One employee stated: 'Overall, I am happy with the working conditions. Some colleagues are not because of the many involuntary redundancies that are taking place throughout the bank. People are afraid of losing their jobs.' The discontent and fear among staff created by the job insecurity makes it impossible for the organisation to motivate its work force to be customer-focused and service-oriented. And yet the Omega Bank is also proceeding with an internal marketing initiative. Now, internal marketing cannot be accommodated in an atmosphere of corporate restructuring and staffing turbulence. The bank needs to realise that if lower-level needs remain unsatisfied, they cannot hope to motivate their staff in terms of higher-level expectations of the type associated with internal marketing.

Overview

Despite the accolades awarded to Alpha Group and the brickbats awarded to Omega, there remain many blocks to the effective implementation of internal marketing that may well have resonance for other banks in other countries, as well as those in Cyprus. These blocks may well forestall marketing effectively taking root in banking organisations and highlight the fact that marketing itself may still be seen as an add-on to real business, or a form of window-dressing (i.e., rhetoric rather than reality).

The majority of Cypriot banks are driven by bureaucracy and by mechanistic structures which are not conducive to creating the 'climate for service' that is a prerequisite in enabling individuals to be customer-focused and service-oriented. The existence of 'red tape' which requires constant adherence to rules and procedures often results in unreasonably slow internal service since it stifles internal suppliers' spontaneity in responding to internal *and external* customers' needs and wants. This creates discontent and decreases motivation among staff *and customers*. The study supports the idea that rule rigidity blocks individuals' willingness to go out of their way to satisfy their customers (internal and external), which creates role stress especially among customer-contact employees who tend to get all the blame and complaints from external customers. The mechanistic structure of banks also results in slow recovery from any service delivery failures.

One branch manager said: 'Things can get very slow and at times we get so much "wrapped up" in our own red tape that we forget that there is an internal or external customer that needs a speedy decision.' A front-line employee said:

> The size of our organisation dictates that we have very clear guidelines as to what we are allowed to do. It's difficult to go out of your way to satisfy a customer ... the bank is all about systems and rules which sometimes create barriers in delivering the level of service your internal and external customers expect. We've got no say in what goes on really, we all have to follow structured guidelines and regulations that are set by the head office. Our internal suppliers find it difficult to provide the level of service that we want because of the rigid policies ... you can ask them for something but, they will say: *it needs to be approved and it will take up to three weeks, it's not up to me.*

Many employees suggest that it is not enough to train and motivate only front-line service providers; both front and back office employees have to be equally motivated to provide a high level of service to the next person in the value chain. In effect, by only affecting the behaviour of front line personnel, internal marketing leads to the creation of a split culture, which marginalises certain types of individuals while simultaneously claiming to empower them.

The evidence suggests that despite the rhetoric surrounding such training programmes, they are often used in a manipulative way. Managers claim that these programmes clearly demonstrate that the organisation cares about the needs and wants of all staff, when in effect it is clear that only front-line staff benefit from most of these courses. Very often, these programmes are launched within the context of internal marketing only in order to signal a more people-oriented management style. However, involvement in these programmes tends to benefit the bottom line of the organisation, mainly through improved staff performance and productivity rather than through improved morale and employee satisfaction. In theory, employees have every opportunity to participate in the development programmes in practice, though this has to be done alongside an already heavy workload. A branch manager claimed:

> the bank expects you to be sales targeted and service targeted and also to juggle with all the other things that we are suppose to be doing. We can't implement some of the internal marketing activities if customers need serving. It's a juggling exercise really; you have to balance it out with everything else that you do. We try to maintain a level of service to our customers whilst the practice of internal marketing requires a certain degree of self-development, which you can't always achieve within the normal working day because of the constraints: for example, telephones and customers. So, the only way you can try to achieve any self-development is outside the normal banking hours, which isn't always acceptable or possible. Therefore, you do find problems in that respect because it is important that staff have that sort of quality time and we can't always do that.

Internal standards are another important element of the internal marketing programmes implemented by many banks. Bank branches appear to set desired levels of quality for internal service encounters. Some branch managers see these standards as vital in ensuring internal service quality. In the words of one bank manager:

> IM is motivating individuals to be customer focused and service oriented, and everything is geared towards that ... our personal targets, our team objectives, the organisational objectives. Everybody is aware of the performance standards. IM emphasises the importance of meeting the service quality standards in order to improve your relationship with your colleagues. You are bound to have an increase in customer service because you are influencing the behaviour of employees on a planned basis. You can easily improve service by highlighting it, rewarding it, and making sure that people understand how the level of service affects the success of the organisation.

Some employees seem to share this perspective. In the words of an employee: 'Everybody is aware of the quality standards and everybody has service quality targets. IM emphasises the importance of meeting the service standards in every internal service encounter.' But there are also dissenting voices, which question the apparent neutrality of service standards. Service standards are thought to be devices in the hands of management by which they attempt to reduce complexity to relatively simple patterns and transform the organisation into a more controllable place. In their attempt to order reality according to their preferred rationality, top management use service standards as lenses through which individuals are viewed, judged, measured and compared against others. Those individuals who do not conform to the prescriptions laid down by these standards are either 'given help' (via training programmes) to adjust their behaviour or are simply pushed away. An employee said:

> We are regularly monitored in terms of the quality of service we provide internally and externally, and the rewards are linked to our performance. IM highlights this link. In implementing IM, we are very 'heavy' on customer service, improving customer service, and meeting the customers' expectations. There are courses within the branch that staff volunteer to go on in order to improve customer service ... we have to nominate a member of the staff, who's performed exceptionally and who deserves some kind of recognition for the quality of customer service they've achieved. We are regularly assessed on our performance towards service targets ... there is pressure to perform exceptionally ... there is always the fear of redundancy so you have to be among the top performers.

As part of the IM initiative most banks were eager to align corporate and individual goals via complex *reward* systems. Banks offered both tangible and intangible rewards for reaching organisational goals. There seemed to be a strong emphasis on the use of monetary rewards, especially for front-line employees (branch managers included), with respect to the opening of new accounts and sales achieved against set targets. Such monetary rewards take the form of bonuses and commissions. One bank uses individual bonuses for customer account managers, personal banking service managers and branch managers to complement the team bonus that is based on the performance of the group in terms of sales and customer service. Another bank has launched personal bonus schemes for staff with a sales responsibility, such as general sales supervisors, branch managers, and savings and investments advisers. Thus, front-line staff have more opportunities to obtain monetary rewards than the back-office staff. The key reason for this is that banks tend to link monetary rewards to quantitative targets, such as sales figures. Since only customer-contact personnel have sales targets, only they have an opportunity to obtain these rewards. One branch manager said: 'We are becoming more sales driven all the time ... IM is used to direct people's efforts towards achieving higher sales. We've got to get the sales targets ... everyone has to achieve the sales targets in order to get the bonuses and a salary increase at the end of the year.' One employee said: 'Sales, definitely sales. This is the key target of our role. Many of the IM activities are aimed in enabling us to be more successful in our selling role: the training, the rewards.'

The most common reward policy for sales personnel is to pay them a fixed annual salary plus a variable commission. A problem with using this method is that a customer-contact employee who aims to maximise his or her commission earnings is often not concerned with the quality of the service-production/delivery process, and thus is not in a position to maximise customer satisfaction and thereby secure repeat business. This reward strategy also discriminates heavily against personnel whose targets cannot be directly linked to sales revenues but whose contribution to providing technical back-up may be equally paramount for the success of the business.

Despite the fact that some banks have launched a reward and recognition campaign targeted at all staff, aiming to build awareness of the 'One Bank' spirit (people united in achieving common goals) and to foster teamwork, the current monetary reward system divides people by creating massive status differences.

The achievement of qualitative targets, such as service quality, is rewarded mainly by intrinsic non-monetary rewards such as gifts, medals and plaques. In certain cases, these may be instigated by head office, but more usually they are left to the branch managers' discretion. What is confusing is the fact that only quantifiable matters seem to be recognised as crucial and therefore rewarded financially (e.g., sales/account openings). Service quality, being intangible, takes a backstage position: a few words of praise, an insignia or a badge with the words 'employee of the month' are supposed to be of sufficient standing to motivate the employees to deliver service quality.

Although claiming to create a cohesive culture around the goal of customer satisfaction, this element of the 'internal marketing mix' seems to work to the contrary. It divides rather than unites, it fosters dissent rather than harmony. An employee said:

> It can get competitive at times, it creates competition amongst people and we get a *negative impact*. It can get *quite divisive* actually. If one person is performing, and you are giving them all the training, the rewards, and the recognition then it can split people up. The monetary rewards create status differences, and dissatisfaction. It can hurt teamwork ... you have to make sure you reward the team as a whole, rather than individuals.

A branch manager claimed:

> In practising IM there is an emphasis on the role of contact personnel which could lead to conflict and discontent. Most of the rewards and recognition are given to front-line personnel. It's not fair ... everybody should be valued. After all this is what IM is all about: acknowledging that all people in all functions have an impact on external customers and treating them as equals. It should be uniting people but instead it divides them because of the emphasis on front line personnel.

The study indicates that branch personnel sometimes experience dissatisfaction in their internal service encounters with internal support departments. The dissatisfaction arises from difficult access and unreasonably slow service delivery. This is surprising given that banks have (apparently) restructured their operations in such a way that the administrative functions and data processing are centralised within internal support departments in order to enable their branch staff to give priority to customer service and personal selling. These unsatisfactory internal service encounters could result in internal customer dissatisfaction. A branch manager said:

> say for instance we decided to promote mortgages, we will need some promotional items to give to customers when they come in. Sometimes it is very difficult to obtain these items, so we need something to be done. The marketing department needs to be more accessible to us, so that I can pick up the phone and say to them ... we are having a mortgage promotion in two weeks, can you send us something? Instead, we have to deal with '*You'll have to order it and it will take six weeks.*' We need to have something better than that.

The study reveals that the there is incongruence between the rhetoric of internal marketing rhetoric and its practice. Even though many Cypriot retail banks have adopted internal marketing in order to achieve competitive differentiation through enhanced customer and service orientation (long-term strategic focus), they have failed to develop a formal and 'holistic' internal marketing implementation approach. Instead, they have adopted a tactical approach. There is a need to adopt internal marketing at a strategic level and then transform it into formal action plans. It is also important that internal marketing is implemented as a 'holistic' management process. It appears that the internal marketing practice within the branch networks is left to the discretion of branch managers:

> There is nothing set in concrete. It's all up to each individual branch what we will achieve and how we will achieve it. You will find that the applicability and success of internal marketing varies between branches of the same bank due to the degree of willingness of the staff to embrace it and the lack of a formal internal marketing programme.

This finding suggests that internal marketing is more like a ritual rather than an important strategy which justifies any investment in terms of money and time. The issue of implementation is perhaps the most significant aspect of internal marketing within banks that needs to be addressed. Both employees and branch managers expressed the need to achieve an organisation-wide sharing of the internal marketing rhetoric in order to contribute to the holistic adoption of internal marketing. An employee said:

> it needs to be adopted by everyone within the organisation ... the internal support departments, the branch managers, the front line ... if we adopt it at a branch level but we don't receive the necessary support and service quality from the head office and the internal units, then we feel let down ... we will seem incompetent in the eyes of customers ... and the bank's reputation will suffer.

The ad hoc approach to the practice of internal marketing is also evidenced by the lack of an effective internal communication system regarding internal marketing. Banks have failed to launch a formally structured and organisation-wide internal communication strategy in terms of:

- attracting staff attention to internal marketing
- maintaining staff interest in its potential benefits
- arousing staff desire to adopt the internal marketing rhetoric
- getting action (implementing the internal marketing activities)

A branch manager supported this, saying:

> [we need] better communication. We need to explain that the people at the front-line of a branch that deal with the bank's customers need better support.

Those people need to be seen as customers so that they can deal more successfully with their customers. The notion of 'internal customers' is always badly
communicated. One of the things that doesn't live up to my expectations always
with our support units, it's their communication … what they can do for us [the
branch]. Very often it can be that their communication is an overstatement of
what they can do.

The lack of a formal internal communication system for internal
marketing within the banks studied has resulted in deficiencies in the
internal marketing practice, which are outlined below:

1   There is a lack of cross-functional participation, integration and
    coordination of the internal marketing practice.

2   There is unsuccessful implementation in terms of ensuring that
    everyone knows what is involved and their role in the whole
    activity.

3   There is inconsistency in the way it is implemented within the
    branch network.

Unless the banks studied recognise that their current internal marketing approach is too abstract and address the need to develop a holistic implementation approach, the efforts and time invested in internal
marketing will be wasted. The results from an effective internal
marketing initiative may never be enjoyed to the maximum.

Summary and conclusion

It appears that the internal marketing practice within Omega Bank
reflects the realities of the economic environment in Cyprus. The
intense competition in the Cypriot financial services sector has been
the source of an emphasis on sales. Traditionally banks have been
sales-oriented, reflecting the culture of the Cypriot society whereby
the banker was predominantly a salesperson 'pushing' products to
uninformed and uneducated consumers. In the case of Omega, the
bank has launched an internal marketing initiative which nourishes
a sales mentality among employees, reflecting their inherited culture.
However, the IM campaign is mis-timed and unfortunate as it comes
directly on the heels of downsizing and the closure of unprofitable
branches. Moreover, consumers have become a lot more educated
and informed, and hence can make better choices and recognise the

forceful and often manipulative attempts of bank personnel to sell in order to get their commissions.

Meanwhile, Alpha Group has recognised that the effective implementation of internal marketing has the potential to improve employee attitudes and the quality of the internal service interactions by demonstrating a 'people-oriented mentality'. In the absence of long-term product and price differentiation, this bank recognises that quality customer service is the only means for gaining sustainable advantage. The practice of internal marketing has the potential to motivate employees to change their attitudes towards external and internal customers and become more customer- and service-oriented. This approach to implementing internal marketing also reflects political realities in Cyprus. The accession of Cyprus to the EU, which has been eagerly anticipated for decades and has been the focal point of political negotiations, has motivated Alpha Group to realise the need to bring about a change in the internal environment in order to move the organisation closer to European standards in the light of forthcoming competition with many reputable and well-established European financial corporations.

Internal marketing seems to be used in the two banks studied as a means to enable staff to understand their role and positioning within the internal customer–supplier chain, with the ultimate aim of achieving outstanding external customer service. An improvement in the customer focus of the organisation is a key element in achieving a marketing orientation. The case study of Omega Bank indicates how a business in Cyprus has adopted the *rhetoric of marketing*, but not translated this into delivering customer satisfaction. By contrast, the case study of Alpha Group has at least attempted to show how a business in Cyprus has delivered the *reality of marketing*: that is, it has found ways to translate the marketing concept in terms of delivering desired customer satisfaction (albeit to an internal audience). There remain, however, some nagging suspicions that the marketing concept still has a long way to go, even in this ostensibly positive example.

It seems that although the idea was to create a strong organisational culture around the values of service quality and customer satisfaction, internal marketing through its four rituals has in fact led to dissent, division and ambiguity in the Omega Bank case. It is clear that despite the strong organisational emphasis on training and development, as well as the notion of 'internal customers' (both of which are fundamental to internal marketing), this bank has failed to deliver the desired benefits in practical terms. Some marketing orientation was evident in the idea of involving staff in making the kinds of internal changes which could be linked to marketplace performance that external customers would value. Hence, there is a clear difference between what the rhetoric promises versus what is actually delivered (i.e., the reality).

Differences really lie in the way banks interpret and practise internal marketing principles (the rhetoric). Specifically, Omega Bank has exhibited an outburst of branch and staff reductions, which has created staff dissatisfaction and low staff morale; a reward structure that creates inequalities and divides staff; low-quality service in internal service encounters, which results in internal customer dissatisfaction; and limited time allowed to staff for training and development.

A service company, such as a bank, can be only as good as its people. A service is a performance and it is usually difficult to separate the performance from the people. With services, internal marketing can pave the way for external marketing. Both banks have realised the need for building people-oriented cultures, which is the best way to meet the wants and needs of internal and external customers when the product is a performance. However, there is a need to ensure that actual practice goes well beyond marketing rhetoric and delivers in reality.

Internal marketing would appear to offer a way forward in terms of marketing reality. It does proffer a forum for purposeful interaction between organisational members as a catalyst for change within the organisation's culture. However, internal marketing is the medium and not the message. If the fundamental principles are wrongly applied and the implementation of the organisation remains incompatible with a marketing orientation then internal marketing programmes will fail. Implementing internal marketing within an organisation in order to achieve desirable marketplace ends is not straightforward or easy. 'Turning the wheel' to internal marketing is not easy, but its successful implementation can produce tremendous payoffs. Certainly, rhetoric is no substitute for reality.

The rhetoric and reality of marketing in New Zealand

lynne eagle

Aims

1 To illustrate actual marketing practice in a small, traditional Western-oriented country faced with twin disadvantages of a small domestic market and at a considerable distance from large international markets.

2 To provide an overview of the impact on marketing operations of a move from a highly regulated economy to one of the world's least regulated economies.

3 To explore the impact of globalisation on the marketing operations of companies active in this market, and on their marketing communications activity in particular.

Introduction

> The marketing concept means that an organization aims all its efforts at satisfying its customers – at a profit. A marketing orientation means trying to carry out the marketing concept. Instead of just trying to get customers to buy what the firm has produced, a marketing-oriented firm tries to offer customers what they need. (Perreault and McCarthy, 1999, p. 34)

However, in the era of globalisation, how does marketing theory translate into practice in small countries? In this chapter, we focus on New Zealand as an example of an economy suffering from two potential handicaps (small size, and considerable distance from major markets) and examine whether the commitment to satisfying the wants and needs of customers extends beyond rhetoric into real marketing practice.

New Zealand is a small, English-speaking country in the south-west Pacific, with a static population of slightly under 4 million, over three-quarters of which live in the North Island, and over one million of these within the main urban area of Auckland (Statistics New Zealand, 2001). Of particular interest is the move from a highly regulated 'protectionist' economy, post-1945, to one of the world's least regulated economies by the late 1990s. Lessons in the New Zealand market can be compared with, or even implemented in, much larger markets, particularly those faced with or undergoing similar deregulatory pressures.

New Zealand's economic history

Historically, New Zealand's economy was centred on agricultural commodity exports with subsidies, protected industries, high taxes, generous social security and a complex range of foreign exchange and financial controls (see Dickson, 1993). Exports, almost exclusively of agricultural commodities, had enjoyed preferential and guaranteed access to British markets since the first 'freezer ship' transported a consignment of frozen lamb to Britain in 1882 (Kelly, 1995; Kennedy, 1999).

What changed?

The shock of Britain joining the EEC in the early 1970s and the loss of preferential status was profound. An even more substantial shock then occurred with a change of government in 1984. The new Labour government abolished import controls and export subsidies, reduced tariffs and floated the exchange rate, as well as liberalising financial and foreign exchange markets. In addition, exogenous factors relating to the globalisation of financial and product markets, described by Kelly (1995, p. 333) as 'colonization by international capital and management' severely affected New Zealand firms. Many state-owned assets were commercialised and then sold, with 79 per cent of ownership going to offshore interests (Gaynor, 1999). The far-reaching nature of the New Zealand market reforms, and particularly the 'blitzkrieg' speed of their implementation (for a detailed discussion, see Kelly, 1995), have been subjected to extensive and often contradictory analysis (see Schick, 1998; Sharp, 1994) regarding benefits or otherwise to New Zealand firms and to the public as a whole.

The outcome, regardless of the debate, was that marketing organisations were faced with a dual challenge: increasing the need to export without subsidies and reacting to the fierce competitive threat from newly deregulated imported products (Chetty and Hamilton, 1996). Notably, from a marketing communication perspective, advertising of newly deregulated imported products grew at a phenomenal rate, forcing New Zealand business leaders to rethink their marketing activities. The consequence was inevitable: a market 'shake-out'. Many did not survive, and those that did often went through substantial operational downsizing.

New Zealand's small domestic market, coupled with the increased competition from imported products, has forced a necessary focus on international markets and on ways to overcome isolation (because of distance) from the main markets of the world. Australia, through its relative closeness to New Zealand in terms of distance, and similarities of population profiles, lifestyle, education and political outlook, has provided a solid but competitive market for New Zealand products. In the 21st century, the rapid development of communications technology enabled New Zealand to join the rest of the world on a more immediate basis. This, coupled with more efficient sea and air freight to global markets, opened up significant opportunities for export-driven marketers who were forced to focus very much on providing what their customers, often from very different cultures, not only wanted but demanded. These marketers were often competing against much larger, better-resourced, international competitors.

Despite these developments, New Zealand's export focus remains somewhat of a contradiction. On the one hand, there is criticism of major (former statutory) marketing boards and the agribusiness industries they represent, despite the deregulation of most sectors in 2001 (Nayga, 1994; Stevenson, 2001). Criticism centres on monopolistic structures stifling innovation and the concomitant slowness in reacting to international market changes. On the other hand, New Zealand IT industries have been applauded for being nimble and flexible, and specialising in small, niche markets (Ein-dor, Myers and Raman, 1997). These are markets in which neither small size nor geographic isolation are economic disadvantages. An example of this is the international award-winning 'Virtual Spectator' software (see Barton, 2001a).

All levels of government see the potential importance of e-commerce to New Zealand marketers as being 'the freezer ship of the 21st Century' (Ministry of Commerce, 1998). While enthusiastic supporters of globalisation proclaim a potential bonanza now that 'the [apparent] tyranny of distance has been obliterated' (Holton, 1998, p. 8), Thurow (1997) offers a more cautionary approach, suggesting that globalisation is just one of many *effects* rather than an actual cause of change. He suggests that technologies and interactions are producing a knowledge-based economy that is changing how all people conduct their economic and social lives (a theme echoed by Schultz and Kitchen, 2000).

The marketing communication environment

In New Zealand, global influences can be seen in many ways, not least the increasing overseas ownership of the main media vehicles. For example, the Canadian Canwest Network owns two of the four major free-to-air network television channels, with approximately 21 per cent market share (A.C. Nielsen, 2001) and also holds some ownership of radio networks. News Ltd hold major shares in news paper, magazine and pay TV activity. Tony O'Reilly holds major shareholdings in newspaper, radio magazines and outdoor advertising. Kerry Packer also controls a substantial part of the lucrative consumer magazine market.

The New Zealand market from a marketer's perspective

A high proportion of global marketers operate in New Zealand. Food, toiletries, pharmaceutical, motor vehicles, oil, finance, insurance, alcoholic and non-alcoholic beverages, toys and other related industries, owned and increasingly directed from multinational and global bases, are represented. This is of evident benefit to the New Zealand marketing communications industry, but there is a downside: while the Association of New Zealand Advertisers Inc. represents over 90 major media advertisers in all industry segments, only 22 per cent of these are predominantly New Zealand-owned and operated. Over 70 per cent have direct operational reporting lines into Australia through regional offices. Increasingly, marketing decisions for New Zealand are being made in Australia, or from a regional headquarters in Asia for the entire Australasian/Pacific region, thus diminishing opportunities for local management input, particularly at a strategic level (Irwin, 2001).

New Zealand as a microcosm

As the New Zealand market mirrors overseas development and the population is generally defined as an 'early adopter' of overseas trends and innovations, it is a preferred test market for many multinationals, not only for products, services, and marketing communications, but equally importantly for executives from overseas. Expatriate middle management and senior executives are frequently given the opportunity for a period of training in New Zealand before being absorbed into positions in other larger markets. This is particularly the case with the marketing discipline. But, while multinational companies also take New Zealand marketers to other markets for training, exceptional managers 'keep on going' in overseas roles and invariably do not return to New Zealand's small market. Those who do not wish to remain overseas find it increasingly difficult to return to New Zealand's shrinking management market.

Drake (2001, p. 1) stresses heightened awareness in major markets such as the USA for the importance of multi-cultural representation and understanding, criticising industry efforts and suggesting that marketing communication practitioners who lack cultural literacy will be hampered in their efforts to help clients sell their products and services to an increasingly diverse consumer groups. But these lessons in cross-cultural communication have been learned by necessity in New Zealand, both in terms of the diversity of the domestic ethnic bases, but more importantly from the experiences gained in exporting to countries with vastly different cultural bases. This therefore represents another area in which 'the New Zealand experience' can aid marketing communications development in much larger markets.

The impact of globalisation on marketing communication

As previously noted, the impact of global marketing is particularly noticeable in New Zealand and an empirical study of New Zealand marketers' perception of the globalisation of marketing communications and the ways in which standardisation and localisation decisions are handled is therefore reviewed here.

Clifton (2001) highlights several major influences on the New Zealand marketing communication industry, including:

- marketing departments and whole head offices based outside Asia and Australia
- downgrading of marketing departments generally (no longer does the Director of Marketing work with the Chief Executive Officer (CEO) and Director of Finance as the company management triumvirate)
- marketing and advertising decisions being made offshore
- commoditisation of media
- commercials being made offshore and adapted for New Zealand's use (with not only cultural issues but legislative/regulatory concerns)
- little investment in brand building

Clifton further notes that the world-wide trend in advertising is for short lead-time, retail-based, call-to-action advertisements. Clients refuse to spend money on anything that does not (to them) lead to instant ringing of cash registers. This puts further pressure on the media, agencies, production facilities, and on the clients themselves. To break this cycle, there is a need for reassessment of the entire marketing communications industry and the role various specialists perform within it. This reassessment is consistent with rethinking the marketing concept and strategic coordination of organisational skills and resources advocated by Kotler in the 1980s with his now famous 'megamarketing' concept (see, e.g., Kotler, 1986; Whalen, 1984). A more recent echo of Kotler's views can be seen in Kitchen and Schultz's (1999, p. 8) critique of current organisational structures that, he suggests, stifle marketing communication success. Both marketers and their marketing communication suppliers need new skills but have not as yet fully embraced the education, training and re-skilling required (e.g., Eagle *et al.*, 1999; Kitchen and Schultz, 1998; Schultz and Kitchen, 2000).

Perceptions of New Zealand marketers regarding globalisation

In a study of the perceptions of senior marketing executives regarding the impact of globalisation on their operations, Kitchen and Eagle (2001) found that globalisation was perceived as a very real and pervasive phenomenon impacting on all areas of business activity both from an internal company perspective and an external market-oriented perspective. The driving forces, according to respondents (see Table 5.1), are:

- communication technology
- the concomitant need to develop integrated communication strategies
- the need to respond to increased globalisation
- the recognised need/desire by consumers to participate in global lifestyles that are perceived as converging

Economic and environmental trends were seen as the least significant, as were channels and distribution. Respondents indicated that distribution channels and methods were seen as adapting and flexing because of, rather than driving, significant changes within the marketing community. The only point that is debatable here is the perception that integrated communication may mean different things to different multinational marketing executives, a point that is not without resonance elsewhere (see Schultz and Kitchen, 2000).

These marketers also recognised that communications, in the 21st century, need to be integrated if only because disparate messages spell potential ambiguity. But while recognition of the essentiality of integration was pronounced – and driven by customer need and corporate exigency – 'saying integration is essential is easy, it's the doing that's causing significant heartburn' (leading board level marketing executive). Thus, the ideal of a range of customers accessing globally communicated products and services in a global market

Table 5.1	Factors impacting on globalisation developments		
Abbreviated Statement tested (ranked by strength of agreement) where 1 = disagree strongly, 5 = agree strongly		Mean	Standard deviation
Communication technology		4.7	0.46
Global consumerism		4.4	0.94
Integrated communication		4.3	0.46
Globalisation of markets		4.3	0.81
Global marketing communication		4.1	0.70
Business process re-engineering		4.1	0.74
Integrated business strategies		4.1	0.85
Consolidation and concentration		4.0	0.65
Internal organisational factors		4.0	0.75
Greater focus on brand communication		4.0	0.75
Prevailing competitive environment		4.0	1.06
Channels and distribution		3.9	0.80
Prevailing environmental circumstances		3.8	0.94
World-wide economic trends		3.7	1.04
Top management objectives		3.7	0.82

was applicable only to a tiny minority of wealthy customers in New Zealand. Where globally integrated communications *were seen to be applicable* was in the business-to-business sector. Thus, the drive for globalisation, insofar as communications were concerned, was occasioned more by corporate edict than individual strategic business requirement; but then, of course, corporate headquarters are in a position to gather data globally.

However, there is still an underlying perception among executives in New Zealand that strategic business units in a specific area or country invariably *prefer* localised, or adapted, communication strategies as these contribute more effectively to the bottom line. Moreover, there is still a widespread acceptance of the view that *in situ* marketers invariably have a deeper understanding of market dynamics than the understanding elicited from a global database. But then, of course, the argument for localised management in terms of communications is the same argument for more autonomy in terms of overall marketing.

Insofar as this study was concerned, *the major drivers of any move towards globalisation were those occasioned by organisational – not environmental – forces.* Corporate headquarters often seek to downsize promotion and communication campaigns, irrespective of whether such campaigns were configured for reception in New Zealand's markets or not. The worldwide increase in advertising production and media space costs naturally spells ostensible advantage in not adapting advertisements. Thus, while executives perceived advantages in terms of greater localisation of marketing communications, these perceptions never went much beyond this.

Strategic business unit executives are unable to adopt a more local perspective for brands as they are driven by corporate edict (i.e., what 'works' elsewhere). Nonetheless, the Internet was perceived to be well suited for international brand building and this was being used wherever possible. Thus marketing communications is 'globally integrated' but the level of development means that this is just a bundling together of promotional mix elements. Note that the inside-out focus means that marketing communications are not focused on the valuation of customers and prospects at the level of individual countries or, for that matter, the all-important customers. Thus relating communications to underlying customer databases, and hence developing sustainable brand relationships, may be far more difficult, in, say, New Zealand than it would be in a much larger marketplace scenario.

As Schultz and Kitchen (2000) point out, the first stage of 'integration' ably positions and delineates much of New Zealand's marketing communication activities. Thus, while there are developed models showing the way forward in terms of developing and implementing globally integrated approaches, often strategic business unit executives may be more focused on simple macro factors, such as market saturation and advertising expenditure, than on customer needs, wants and relationship marketing approaches. It is interesting that the power shift from manufacturers to retailers is not seen as a major driver, perhaps reflecting the reassessment of the distribution chain being undertaken by many organisations as a consequence of new electronic commerce opportunities. Samiee (1998, p. 16) suggests channel intermediaries 'must constantly economically justify their presence in the channel, otherwise other channel members will eventually bypass the structure or develop their own, more efficient channels and processes'.

Case I: health insurance: failure to meet customer expectations and failure to deliver customer satisfaction

The following case illustrates how neglecting basic marketing principles can result in substantial (and probably long-term) credibility problems for marketers. It illustrates an area in which the rhetoric of satisfying the customer's needs – in this case, comprehensive medical insurance at minimal cost – is tempered very much by the world-wide realities of ever-increasing costs for the provision of medical insurance services. Publicly funded health care in New Zealand, as in most other countries, is subject to various forms of rationing. A perpetual gap exists between supply and demand of health services, with waiting lists and 'points' (based on the severity of a medical condition) being used to determine treatment priorities. Private health care, itself using price as a rationing device, offers an alternative to public waiting lists and also control over medical specialist selection. Healthcare insurance has been a major, if controversial, growth area, outlaying $561 million in healthcare costs on behalf of policyholders in the year ended 30 June 2000 (Health Funds Association, 2002).

Health insurance premiums have more than doubled in the past decade, with a corresponding decline in the number of policyholders from approximately half of all New Zealanders in the early 1990s to only one-third in the most recent year (Weir, 2001). A substantial part of the decline in policy numbers can be attributed to a world-wide trend. When economies were booming up to the early 1990s, employers were prepared to pay for staff benefits, such as subsidised (or fully funded) health insurance, in order to attract and retain workers. With economies struggling in the latter part of the 1990s – and continuing to struggle in the new millennium – employers both reduced staff benefits and the overall size of their work forces. Individuals are financially unwilling or unable to cover all of the costs of private medical insurance themselves, falling back on public services (McCarthy, 2002).

The New Zealand health insurance market has seen numerous mergers and acquisitions, the latest being the market leader, 40 year old Southern Cross, taking over Aetna NZ in 2001, after winning an appeal against a Commerce Commission ruling that the acquisition would result in over dominance of the industry (New Zealand Newspapers Association, 2001). After the takeover, Southern Cross held some 80 per cent of the market. The next largest competitor, Tower Health, who had previously taken over Axa Health, held some 11 per cent and Sovereign (owned by one of the largest banks) held most of the balance. Numerous small industry specific schemes exist, such as a police health scheme (Health Funds Association,

2002). The market is competitive and, to a certain extent, also commodified, with similar products being offered by all providers. Policyholders are able to claim back a range of medical costs, including general practitioners' visits, prescription costs and specialist consultations. High-cost procedures, such as surgery in a private hospital, can be pre-approved and the costs paid direct by insurance companies to the service provider, thus relieving patients of substantial financial burdens incurred in initially meeting costs then seeking reimbursement.

Central to the Aetna takeover was the acquisition of Aetna's sophisticated computer system. This coincided with a major restructuring and relocation of the claims processing centre from Auckland to Hamilton (a provincial city less than one-fifth of the size of Auckland). Many experienced claims staff were made redundant as a result of the move. However, in late 2001, problems with delays of six weeks or more in settling claims were reported and a major public relations disaster was evident by late January 2002 (O'Sullivan and Gifford, 2002). Problems initially attributed to the new computer system were later revealed to be as much related to the lack of adequate numbers of trained staff to handle the new system. The subsequent resignation of the managing director was announced at the same time as intentions to raise premiums by at least 15 per cent (Sheeran, 2002). While the magnitude of the increase was comparable to increases already announced by the two major competitors, the timing of the announcement did nothing to help perceptions of the company, especially when the competitors were stressing their aim to pay claims within 48 hours (Talbot, 2002).

Further adverse publicity was gained, and relationships with medical specialists and private hospitals – key stakeholders in the provision of medical services – severely damaged when it was reported in the media that Southern Cross was paying claims on time for treatment at hospitals it owned or at those with fixed-price contracts, negotiated in an effort to force down charges, in place (New Zealand Press Association, 2002). Although there have been several reports of Southern Cross health members looking at changing to other insurance providers, those with existing health conditions may find problems in obtaining affordable equivalent coverage from alternative providers. Conversely, Southern Cross could, if it does not restore public confidence, lose its most profitable (low claiming) members and be left with those who are likely to make higher claims and thus be less profitable, further hindering the company's ability to meet the needs or expectations of their customers..

Southern Cross appears to have failed to understand the consumer perception of the benefits (including prompt payment of claims) expected by policyholders (see, e.g., Bateson and Hoffman, 1999) and not to have considered the implications of simultaneously converting to a complex new computer system and relocating the claims processing centre. There also appears to have been a failure to evaluate the impact of regular rate increases (well above the rate of inflation). The decline in policy numbers in the last decade indicates that there is substantial price sensitivity in this sector and sends a very clear signal that this provider at least is not delivering what consumers believe they need.

The payment delays, coupled with preferential treatment of their own hospitals, have clearly soured relationships with several key stakeholder groups. In spite of brave announcements of planned innovative insurance products (using the new computer system to reduce costs) and age-related new pricing policies to match premium levels to likely health risks (O'Sullivan and Gifford, 2002), it is clear that Southern Cross's credibility has suffered substantial damage, with potential loss of market share, a change to its membership profile and possibly a further reduction in the number of overall policy holders nationally. There are therefore serious implications for both Southern Cross and for the health insurance industry as a whole.

Case 2: creating real satisfaction from virtual cutting-edge technology

This case illustrates how an information technology provider, eschewing formal marketing plans and overt embracing of marketing concept rhetoric, still focused on providing services that customers wanted. Virtual Spectator began in 1995 with a joint venture between Dunedin-based Animation Research and Auckland-based Terabyte Interactive (i.e., two partners geographically several hundred miles apart) to produce on-screen animations to complement television sports coverage. Terabyte itself was a joint venture partner with Newscorp, investigating options for commercially viable Internet communications media, and in particular pay services. The public first became aware of Virtual Spectator when 'the on screen graphics in the America's Cup yacht racing TV coverage transformed boring pictures of yachts inching across the waves into a sport that was exciting to watch' (Barton, 2001b). The America's Cup series, while featuring top international match racing teams, was unlikely to gain major international television time. In addition, being held in geographically isolated New Zealand, the event thus presented additional challenges for major sponsors needing to find ways to communicate with international media. Internet coverage provided a multimedia-based virtual environment in real time. The success of the concept is evident in the 85,000 people from 151 countries who signed up for the Internet subscription service, with 58,000 giving their credit card and paying for a full subscription (Meek, 2002).

Yachting, however, remains a niche sport. Sports with wider appeal, such as golf, cricket and motor rallying, were then added, providing computer game-like animations in tandem with 'real' pictures and commentary. In addition to television coverage, an Internet-based subscription service for motor-rallying events began in 2001 as a joint venture with the organisation owning television and commercial rights. Motor rallying is regarded as having a high profile globally. Virtual Spectator's coverage is based on segmentation of the world by language, the common underpinning 'culture' being the interest in motor sports and the common customer desire being for current, comprehensive and 'state of the art' race coverage. Coverage is localised to meet the needs of broadcasting rights holders and sponsors/advertisers.

Further expansion into the music industry now enables fans to watch virtual live or archived concerts on their personal computers (PCs). Fans are able to create their own events by cutting between different camera angles or watching from the wings. The music division is positioned to complement rather than compete with music retailers, encouraging fans to buy performing groups' albums (Nikiel, 2001).

Traditional marketing planning with written plans established many months in advance does not fit well with a rapidly changing new medium. However, this does not imply an undisciplined approach. On-going surveys are undertaken with current audiences in order to seek to determine how subscribers perceive the services provided and to gain feedback regarding ways in which future products and services might be developed to meet the needs of specific customer groups. The research also seeks to build an understanding of the way subscribers use and navigate interactive content – particularly as 2½ hours is spent on-line at any time using the Virtual Spectator platform – in order to continually improve or fine-tune existing products and services.

Like many dot.coms, start-up costs have been high and profits elusive. Some $15 million has been invested, starting with private investment and a $300,000 Technology New Zealand (i.e., government) grant. This was followed by substantial US venture capital. The New Zealand company is now a subsidiary of a US registered company to take advantage of more favourable venture capital accounting rules and to make overseas investment more attractive. Some 15 per cent of shares are reserved for present and future staff; such a move is not common in New Zealand, but is specifically designed to attract and hold talented staff.

The case illustrates, among many other features, how technology has overcome many of the distance problems that have plagued New Zealand's companies in the past. A senior executive observes:

> We've already proved we can do our development work where we are. I mean, you've got someone living up a goat track in Sicily watching the America's Cup in NZ on a computer, via a product made by someone living in Dunedin working over the Internet with someone living in Auckland – so who gives a damn where we live? (Grant, 2000)

Summary and conclusion

There are several factors affecting marketing practice in New Zealand. While there is little to forestall globalisation here, there are in fact many barriers militating against marketing strategies – and marketing communications – that are effectively focused on consumer needs. Global strategies for 'traditional'/established companies are driven more by corporate edict than consumer requirements in New Zealand. There is evidence of difficulties in translating the rhetoric of marketing and of integrated communications into effective reality. How common these problems are in other countries remains to be seen.

The biggest challenges faced by the New Zealand industry are, first, the need to turn around the market, refocusing marketers on the value of brand building, and on real brand investment rather than mere cost savings. The current globalisation environment and focus on the (short-term) bottom line are likely to work against this.

Second, there is the need to create new opportunities, capitalising on unique niche products and services. Complacency and clinging to traditional rhetoric, methods and assumptions can be an extremely dangerous path to walk. Seeing the market through consumers' eyes and involving consumers in the product development process calls for rapid reactions, lateral thinking and, at times, a high level of risk taking. Convoluted reporting lines to corporate control centres, the need to conform to corporate edicts and limited local autonomy (and resources) again work against this for many organisations. Potentially, however, the rewards are significant and companies that embrace this latter perspective are proving that they can compete effectively on the global stage.

The rhetoric and reality of marketing in South Korea

dongjin yoon and ilchul kim

Introduction

'The limit of my language is the limit of my world', wrote Ludwig Wittgenstein (1921). This statement becomes even more true when subjects are communicated and disseminated across different languages and different cultures. For example, if a term or a concept were to migrate abroad to where it had never before existed, it would probably be understood differently from its original meaning. For instance, do Westerners really understand 'Zen'? There are perhaps very few Westerners who understand the real meaning of 'Zen', and those who think they may understand probably have different interpretations of the meaning. The analogy holds true with the application of the concept of marketing in Korea. When S.R. Oh published *Marketing Principles* for the first time in Korea in 1963, he defined 'marketing' in the same manner as the National Association of Marketing Teachers (NAMT) did in 1935. Until very recently Korean textbooks and articles adopted a concept and definition of marketing transposed directly from the USA, as defined by the American Marketing Association and Philip Kotler (Chae, 1985). The academic field had been moving slowly in Korea as there had not been much need for marketing up until 1963. Until that time Koreans were more concerned about survival and escaping from starvation due to the serious shortage of commodities after the Korean War. There was no need for the marketing of products in this environment. For 35 years Korea was a Japanese colony, since Japan had taken complete control of Korea and governed it for its own interests.

In 1945, with the defeat of Japan in the Second World War, the Communists took over northern Korea, with the help of the USSR, while the south remained staunchly anti-Communist, supported by the USA and the West. Like most developing countries, the development of the Korean economy was closely linked to its political stability. The last half century can be divided into four stages chronologically, with each stage depicting how marketing principles advanced as a result of changes in the political structure.

Stage 1: 1945–60

The first stage covers the time period from 1945 to 1960. After 1945 many attempts were made to bring Korea together as one country. However, the separate political forms of government in the north and the south made it impossible, eventually leading to the Korean War in 1950 when the north invaded the south. South Korea remained subject to political unrest and, because of its history, was not ready for any form of capitalism. In 1960 an Army General, Chungee-Park, took power through a military coup. The country remained in chaos given all that happened in a relatively short period of time since it had became a nation in 1948. Only one thing concerned most people at this time and that was how to survive starvation. There was no necessity for, or understanding of, marketing at this first stage.

Stage 2: 1961–79

The second stage continued for almost 20 years up until 1980. It was then that General Doowhan-Chun seized control of Korea after the Chief of the KCIA killed President Park. Korea displayed rapid economic growth, from 8 to 10 per cent each year under Park's strong dictatorship. Marketing began to be introduced and studied in universities and schools but there still was no real necessity for it from a business viewpoint since most businesses were export driven, controlled by the government and based on low labour costs.

Stage 3: 1980–97

The third stage was from 1980 to 1997 when Korea encountered a heavy economic recession, the so-called IMF (International Monetary

Table 6.1		The application of marketing in Korea	
Stage	Period	Core value	Marketing perspective
1	1945–60	Survival	No marketing concept
2	1961–79	Growth	Government driven
3	1980 97	Own brand	Rhetoric-driven marketing
4	1998 present	Strategic approach	Reality-driven marketing

Fund) crisis. Supported by the academic community, companies tried to adapt marketing to fit their businesses, but the results can be guessed since marketing was really just a form of rhetoric, unaccompanied by any real move to customer orientation.

Stage 4: 1998 to the present day

The last few years prior to the millennium represent the fourth stage and this was the time when real marketing activity started to take place. These four stages of progression are shown in Table 6.1.

Hunger demand (1945–60): no marketing period

The Korean War (1950–53), coming just after the 35 years (1910–45) of Japanese domination, left nothing behind but ruins. All efforts were concentrated on survival and there was no need for strategy. People merely followed their instincts. There was no infrastructure and there was a real shortage of commodities, allowing only for the manufacture of simple necessities such as soap and toothpaste. Many relied on goods from relief agencies. The GNP per capita was under US$100. There was no discussion anywhere about marketing during this period, although some universities did use marketing textbooks, literally translated from Japanese (originally from English). Many young scholars, who had left Korea in the early 1950s in order to study in America, had now completed their studies and began to return to Korea to teach marketing exactly as they had learned it while abroad. This, however, was no more than an introductory level and this was indeed the introductory period where marketing was perceived to be mainly irrelevant to the needs of businesses and the general population.

Can-do spirit (1961–79): the focus on volume sales

By May of 1960, national chaos was calming down following the success of General Chungee-Park's coup. The new government eliminated the National Assembly and suspended the Constitution. The government determined investment priorities and the business territories of major companies (later called *chaebol*). All kinds of union activities were prohibited. There were two remarkable policies determined and driven by the strong government. The domestic infrastructure started to change, moving from one of agriculture to industrial production under the slogan of the 'New Village Movement' (an idea borrowed from Denmark), and strong export-driven policies were implemented based on competitive labour costs. Trading businesses were encouraged with various benefits such as tax deductions, low interest bank loans and funding. All these were the foundation for a series of '5-year economic development plans', which began in 1961 and lasted into the 1980s. During this period, the Korean economy was growing by at least 8–10 per cent annually, but most of the export products were primarily consumer and OEM (original equipment manufacturer) goods. Companies were evaluated by the government based on the quantity of goods exported. As we mentioned, the domestic market was arranged by product categories as dictated by the government. For example, the home appliances market was occupied by Goldstar Electronics (hereinafter Goldstar), and Samsung Electronics was forced to export rather than compete in the local market. Automobiles and the construction industry market were controlled by Hyundai. It took Daewoo a long time to join the auto and shipbuilding industry. This resulted in monopoly and oligopoly situations. Due to this market situation, there was no room or need for a marketing approach until economic growth began to slow due to the maturing of the domestic market, and the export market started to slow in the late 1970s. Companies began to feel the need to establish their own brands in the international market as the local market matured. The first marketing book in Korea, *Marketing Principles*, was written by Professor Oh and published in 1963 (Chae, 1985; Kim *et al.*, 1996). Due to the short history of this type of study, most articles just introduced foreign theories or hypotheses (Kim, 2000). The driving force behind economic growth during this period was the 'can-do spirit' promoted by the government.

The move towards quality (1980–97): the rhetoric of marketing

The 20 years of military dictatorship ended in 1979 when President Park was assassinated by one of his trusted followers, J.K. Kim (president of the KCIA), in 1979. Though Park was considered a dictator, he was still responsible for moving Korea from the status of an underdeveloped country, where people were concerned about survival, to a more progressive, developing country. Though his strong leadership raised the visible quality of life, there still continued to be many problems.

When President D.W. Chun took over through another military coup in 1980 it was determined that the world had changed too much to maintain Park's style of governing. The government did not have enough power to control businesses and the unions. The GATT (General Agreement on Tariffs and Trade) advantage, like the GSP (Generalised System of Preferences), stopped, and the ITC (International Trade Commission) of the US government imposed anti-dumping duties which affected major export items such as colour televisions, steel and semiconductors. Companies that were unionised were now dealing with significant unrest given the fact that wages had only risen twice in just 10 years. Export companies began to recognise the importance of brands and branding, and major conglomerates such as Daewoo and Samsung turned their eyes towards the mature domestic market. Lucky-Goldstar, the parent company of Goldstar Electronics, had established its credo as 'human harmony' (*Inhwa* in Korean) but changed it to 'value invention for customers' after it lost its number one position in home appliances to Samsung Electronics. For Goldstar, however, the credo was just that: a credo, with no underlying commitment to marketing save as a form of rhetoric or words.

In February 1990, when the Lucky-Goldstar Business Group changed its own credo to one apparently focusing on customers, thousands of other companies started Customer Satisfaction (CS) campaigns. Although they ostensibly became concerned with the needs and wants of consumers, most did not understand exactly what needed to be done to meet consumers' expectations as up until this time they had been enjoying a 'seller's market'. On the other hand, consumers' needs and requirements escalated higher and higher. The Seoul Olympic Games in 1988 and Daejeon Expo in 1993 raised people's expectations to an international level, which was a stage beyond what their supplying companies could achieve at that time.

Meanwhile, management and academia were also increasing awareness of marketing. In the 1990s alone, 2,933 articles were published on marketing and this was almost three times as many as the 1,079 articles during the previous three decades (Kim, 2000). In spite of this growth, many scholars in management were sceptical of the benefits associated with marketing as a concept, and as a business philosophy (Kim, 2000).

The real issue here was that Korea was attempting to catch up with two centuries of the history and development of Western capitalism in under 30 years. Most theories or concepts associated with business practice require time for assimilation and application, and the immature theory and practice of marketing during this period was still no more than a form of rhetoric which may indeed work for a while until better alternatives become available.

The global game (1998–present): real marketing

When several Asian countries crashed into the severe economic recession of the late 1990s, Korea was at the very centre of the chaos. It was considered the worst situation Korea had encountered throughout her 5,000-year history. All efforts were made to correct this 'national crisis'. There was a civilian voluntary gold collection campaign designed to pay back the IMF which drew the attention of foreign correspondents and journalists. But, also during this period, many Korean companies stepped forward to embrace marketing and to embark upon real marketing campaigns. They began systematically to really focus on customers and their needs. One example was a 'recall system' by major auto companies. Many large companies began restructuring and downsizing on their own without government intervention. Non-profit organisations even began to employ marketing techniques. President D.J. Kim regarded himself as national CEO and appeared on a commercial film entitled 'Buy Korean'. Many corporations run by the government were sold or merged. There were many instances of practical and productive cooperation between academia and business and there were some real marketing success stories involving products or services in the domestic market. As Kohli and Jaworski (1990) pointed out, though there are many limits to the implementation of real marketing concepts based on the ideal policy (whatever this may mean), there are significant differences caused by the political, economic and cultural environment.

We now introduce two marketing cases showing how each began to implement marketing techniques for very different reasons and with different results.

Case 1: Goldstar – Korean style but rhetorical in nature

Goldstar Electronics, founded in 1958, was a pioneer in the Korean electronics industry. It had always possessed an innovative management team that in the mid-1980s proved itself to be very capable of handling the transition from a 'seller's to a buyer's market'. Goldstar acknowledged the importance of marketing and placed a priority on customer satisfaction. That is why they changed their credo to 'value invention for customers', following a McKinsey Management Consulting study in 1990. As a result they began to emphasise quality rather than quantity. They reinforced their marketing by extending their nation-wide service and delivery system. It took a while longer for Goldstar to change internally, but they immediately began to communicate their new philosophy and began trying to change the attitudes of the rest of their management team and employees. Below, we review Goldstar's history chronologically showing how they evolved their marketing concept from the rhetoric stage into real marketing, eventually changing their company name to LG Electronics in 1995. Goldstar is a story of how a company tried to evolve a marketing concept into a real marketing story. Their progress was highlighted in a book that included success stories about world-class products such as flat-monitor television and air-conditioners (J.R. Lee, 2000).

Goldstar produced radios, cassette players, fans, refrigerators, black and white television sets, and so on. Initially, they had West German and Japanese financial and technological backing. Domestic disposable income began to improve in 1961, when the Korean government's five-year economic development plan began to show results. Goldstar's sales volume began to show tremendous increases as shown in Table 6.2.

In the 1960s imports were tightly controlled and Goldstar had a share of over 40 per cent of the domestic market. It was a seller's market and sales were not a challenge, but funding growth and

Table 6.2   Goldstar's increasing sales volume

Year	Korean Won	US$
1965	1.28 billion	200,000
1970	7.1 billion	1 million
1975	45.06 billion	38 million

Source: Goldstar (1993), p.264.

Table 6.3   Goldstar's sales trend

	1960	1970	1980	1990	1992
Sales (million Won)	240	7,104	252,992	2,984,019	3,787,450
Export (million US$)	N/A	3.7	155.9	2,088.9	2,555.4

Source: Goldstar (1993).

developing new technologies were the primary concern for management. For example, when Goldstar produced black and white television sets for the first time in Korea in 1966 with Hitachi technology, they could not meet market demand (Goldstar, 1993).

Goldstar enjoyed this seller's market until the market began to get more competitive when the Electronic Industry Promotion Law was enacted in 1968. They tried various things to maintain their dominant market share. They started by enhancing their sales efforts with such things as sales exhibits in 1965, strengthening in-store service departments in 1971, implementing Point of Purchase (POP) advertising in 1972, and initiating dealer promotions in 1973. They expanded their 100 national dealerships to 675 by 1980, and improved product availability and service for customers. However, the customer service part of this effort primarily covered repairing products after they were purchased. While these efforts helped maintain their competitive position domestically, the company itself continued to grow and prosper as the Korean government's five-year economic plan began to accelerate. These economic plans made the exporting of products to the USA a very attractive and lucrative alternative for growth. Goldstar started to export radios to the USA in 1962, and their export volume increased from US$3.7 million in 1970 (see Table 6.3) to US$630 million in 1985.

However, this export boom was not going to last forever and Goldstar knew that it had to improve its long-term domestic market position. The steps they had taken towards consumer marketing up to this point were only small ones. Without any real strategy in place at this time (1975), they began to do some preliminary market research concerning customer attitudes and brand preferences.

The challenge of change

Goldstar maintained its dominant market position both domestically and in the export market until the mid-1980s, but over 60 per cent of their exports relied upon OEM sales. In the late 1980s Goldstar began to encounter real business problems. Various internal challenges (such as union strikes and managerial inertia) and external challenges (such as the opening of the Korean market to imports), coupled with domestic market saturation, resulted in Goldstar losing its leading market position.

Major union strike

In 1984, Goldstar's profits fell below their rivals, Samsung. Matters worsened in 1987 when the company was faced with a major union strike, stimulated by a nation-wide democratic movement and the long history of the company being managed by centralised bureaucrats. These union conflicts caused many problems. For example, in 1989, the production lines stopped for 251 days in four major facilities, losing over US$3 million in expected sales and causing many delivery and quality problems. During this same period, the average wage level of workers rose by over 20 per cent.

Open import markets

The Korean home appliance market was a large market controlled by three major domestic manufacturers: Goldstar, Samsung and Daewoo Electronics. In 1989 the Korean government implemented a new and more liberal import policy, making it more attractive for foreign companies to sell their products in Korea. Foreign companies invested in distribution systems and the import duty on home appliances declined from 30 per cent to 12 per cent between 1988 and 1991. Goldstar knew what the result would be of this new foreign competition, having seen what happened in Taiwan where Japanese imports had caused domestic companies' share to decline from 60 per cent to 20 per cent.

Domestic market saturation

The domestic home appliance market, including such things as colour television sets, video cassette recorders (VCRs), refrigerators, washing machines and microwave ovens, had become a market that was very competitive, as well as very saturated. Demand was slowing considerably since 90 per cent of households already owned these appliances. As the three major manufacturers continued to push to achieve annual sales goals, competition became serious and strong push strategies were used with suppliers which negatively impacted prices, leaving the distribution system in chaos and product quality deteriorating.

H.J. Lee was nominated in 1989 to be the new CEO of Goldstar. He implemented various innovative management approaches such as TPC (Total Productivity Control) and Mind Change Movement, and restructured the organisation to cope with this challenge. Much of this had little positive impact, resulting in a lot of talk but not much action. However, during this time it should be noted that the company, with the help of McKinsey Consulting, began looking towards consumers for answers, and they changed their motto to 'value invention for customers' (see Table 6.4) from the old 'human harmony' motto they had been using.

Customer satisfaction campaign

The major concern for Goldstar in the attempted movement from marketing rhetoric to marketing reality was, 'What should we do

Table 6.4 Core of 'value invention for customers'	
	Direction
Customer	Customer-based decision-making Learn from customer Grow with customer
Value	Support customer Reserve social value (excluding environment protection)
Invention	Innovation, one step ahead World top class
Source: LG Electronics (1995), p.486.	

Table 6.5 Customer satisfaction index (1992)

	General satisfaction	Major items[a]	Customer contact
Goldstar	73.3	76.6	76.6
Competitor	72.5	75.6	74.1

[a] The basis of comparison was the following product categories: colour televisions, video recorders, refrigerators, washing machines.

Source: LG Electronics (1995), p.613.

first to satisfy the customer?' Even though they still had no overall strategy, they summoned all their resources to focus on this issue. First, Goldstar held a nation-wide dealer meeting. At this meeting they presented their new management philosophy of becoming more customer-driven. To reinforce this new direction they conducted various kinds of market research in 1992, trying to understand the consumer as well as trying to find new market opportunities. For example, they conducted comparison studies by selecting 300 users of both Goldstar and Samsung items such as colour televisions, VCRs, refrigerators and washing machines. The outcomes from the study are shown in Table 6.5 which remarkably, and despite the preceding losses in market share, shows that Goldstar was not doing as badly (at least on these criteria) as they feared.

Their first step in trying to move from a push to pull strategy was to extend coverage from their wholesalers to their retailers. They adapted a new corporate identification concept to enhance their image and unify their distributors. Sales management was restructured and they began holding meetings with distributors to find out customers' needs. They also conducted blind product tests to understand product strengths and weaknesses. Notebook computers were provided to all the sales staff and a flexible work system was used to maximise the support of distributors in order to provide the product on demand. Sales incentive programmes were also implemented to motivate the sales team. At this time they began to do more than just talk. Three major marketing programmes were implemented: after-sales service, a customer month event and logistical improvements.

After-sales service
At this time the consumer's voice became louder, demanding improved after-sales service. To meet this demand, Goldstar

increased service manpower. They each drove vehicles and each vehicle carried the latest corporate campaign slogan such as 'visit and service' (1987), 'proactive service' (1988), 'consumers can be secure in their beliefs' (1989), 'Goldstar service as good as the product' (1990). Since 1990, with the vision of making every customer a life-time customer, Goldstar has announced three strategies and seven action plans but, unfortunately, their company infrastructure is still not organised or capable of delivering on this enthusiasm.

Customer month event
Beginning in 1992 Goldstar declared every April to be 'Customer Month', and that year alone they invited 77,586 customers to 203 events. Management met the customers directly to listen to their comments and complaints for the first time. They conducted customer research and found out that consumers did not think the company cared about them (51.6 per cent), that the company was too cen-tralised in its decision-making (32.7 per cent), and that customers did not think the company could meet their expectations (15.7 per cent). Special gifts and promotions were provided during these customer event months. Even employees were mobilised to improve public relations. They became involved with charities, environmental protec-tion issues and blood donation efforts to improve the company's image and to get closer to the customer. The company began to spon-sor concerts and cultural events. Despite all these activities the com-pany still lacked a logical strategic marketing focus.

Logistics improvement
Another customer service challenge for Goldstar was how to deliver products to the distribution centres and to the customers on time. The problem became worse with the rapid increase of automobiles on the road in the 1980s. Maintaining appropriate stock levels is one of the key issues for the home appliance business because of the bulk nature of the product and the high unit price. Goldstar aimed to set up a 24-hour delivery system to all nation-wide distributors. The goal of a 95 per cent service level was achieved in 1995 through 16 logistics centres. The real problem was how properly to balance production goals and sales goals under this self-supporting system.

Towards the reality

These changes for Goldstar resulted in many improvements in their management but, despite their efforts, no real innovation had resulted. Corporate philosophies and campaign slogans were well intended but changed frequently, resulting in some positive actions but none of them lasting and none of them resulting in a real marketing emphasis. It was a new paradigm for most of those involved with Goldstar. Most of the resistance came from middle management personnel, many of whom were still living in the past when their business was growing with little competition. Top management's philosophy could not reach front-line employees due to this bottleneck. The seriousness of the problem can be seen in the extract below, taken from an article written by a staff member in the *Goldstar House Organ* (1991):

> Goldstar will never catch up to our competitors without seriously correcting their internal problems. 'Value creation for customers' means that we have been too wrapped up in creating our own image and we have to confess that we've been ignoring our customers who should be our number one concern. Goldstar is spoiled and full of flatterers. If the company's announcement of a successful service campaign is true, why haven't profits improved?

In most organisations, middle management is the toughest and last group to change. Goldstar, however did attempt to reshape itself through restructuring and began to move in the right direction. It has so far taken over a decade and the utilisation of many resources to begin moving in the right direction, but Goldstar still has a long way to go. Undoubtedly, what this case illustrates is the movement from production to sales orientation, with an attempt being made to dress the latter up as a marketing orientation. As seen here, however, it is no more than a form of rhetoric, which may *in due course* turn towards a more realistic appreciation and application of the marketing concept in a realistic manner.

Case 2: Mando – David against Goliath

The *Kimchi* (pickled vegetable) refrigerator market has grown to become the largest market among white goods in Korea in just a few years. In 2002, its market size was bigger than the colour television market which had been the biggest segment of the electronics market (S.H. Lee, 2001). Housewives used to use normal refrigerators to keep *Kimchi* fresh before the Mando Climate Control Corporation (hereinafter Mando) introduced the *Kimchi*-only refrigerator in 1995. This was a brand new product when it was originally developed, so Mando utilised a test market prior to launch. They chose 3,000 female opinion leaders to use the *Kimchi* refrigerator free for six months. Mando sold 650,000 units in 2001 representing 55 per cent of the total Korean market and became the leading brand. H.K. Hwang, the president of Mando, stated:

> *Kimchi* is one of the major foods for all Koreans but due to changing lifestyles, people moving into apartments, it was difficult for housewives to keep *Kimchi* fresh. [In a typical house, housewives dig a hole in the garden and bury the *Kimchi* jar to keep it fresh during the winter season, but this is not an option in an apartment.] Dimchae [brand name for Mando's Kimchi refrigerator and original name of Kimchi] serves to relieve housewife stress. (S.H. Lee, 2001)

The sushi refrigerator in Japan, why not?

The *Kimchi* refrigerator originated when Mando started to diversify its business in the early 1990s. Mando's original business was as a manufacturer of car radiators and air conditioners, which they supplied to Hyundai Motors, beginning in October 1962. As a manufacturer and supplier of car parts, their sales were contingent upon the success of the companies they supplied within the automobile industry. To improve their business and reduce their reliance on a few automobile manufacturers, Mando developed home use air conditioners in 1994 and sales grew to a point where they achieved number three in the market. Even though they were successful at diversifying from their original industrial business, most of the sales of air conditioners still occurred in the summer. As a result, they had to stop their manufacturing lines for several months during the year. To maintain their rate of production during the winter months and to keep their 800 employees and facilities fully utilised, Mando began manufacturing heating fans, vending machines, boilers, and so on but they were not able to do so efficiently. A new research and development (R&D) team was given the task of dealing with the problem. They decided that there was a market for a *Kimchi* refrigerator. Standard refrigerators from abroad were designed to keep Western-style food fresh but they were not appropriate for fermenting foods such as *Kimchi*.

Like the sushi refrigerator in Japan and the wine refrigerator in France, the Mando R&D team decided that certain foods needed special conditions for optimum preservation. They began to study the problems with keeping *Kimchi* fresh using normal refrigerators. They worked out the best conditions for keeping *Kimchi* at optimum quality, such as temperature and timing, and learned through repeated testing and from cuisine professionals. The R&D team actually formulated their own *Kimchi*, using over 10,000 heads of cabbages, and eventually developed a high-quality product which they then began trying to preserve. They designed some unusual elements into their refrigerator such as putting the door of the *Kimchi* refrigerator on the top rather than on the front like traditional refrigerators. This helped stabilise the inside temperature at $+1$ or -1 degrees centigrade, which provided the best conditions for *Kimchi*. The new product was given the brand name 'Dimchae' – an old name for *Kimchi* in Korea – and was launched in November 1995. (Traditionally Koreans make a special *Kimchi* called 'Kimjang Kimchi' just before winter sets in.)

Launching the *Kimchi* refrigerator

The '*Kimchi*-only refrigerator' was a brand-new concept and the company name 'Mando', given their past industrial business, was not well known to consumers. As a result, when they launched their product it generated little interest because of low awareness of the company. Since they had invested so much money in R&D and in product development they had limited financial resources and could not conduct a large-scale national advertising campaign. Their 180 franchise outlets were also not familiar to the consumer. Based on the test marketing result, Mando adapted a non-mass approach rather than mass marketing at the launching stage. First, they selected 3,000 women opinion leaders including non-governmental organisation leaders, popular chefs, parent–teacher association members and even politicians, letting them use the product free for six months. After that, if they chose, they could purchase the unit at a 50 per cent discount. Mando found that 97 per cent of the users in this test market were satisfied with the refrigerator and the way it maintained the quality of *Kimchi*. In the first year, 4,000 units were sold.

The next step was to create a word-of-mouth advertising campaign. The first 4,000 purchasers, including major opinion leaders, talked about their experiences. Mando hired and trained women to go door-to-door. They asked them to demonstrate the product at prearranged gatherings of women in their homes. Through this direct selling strategy, Mando sold 20,000 units during the second year. In their third year, 1997, the Korean economy entered into a recession because of the foreign currency shortage (the so-called IMF crisis). Mando did not let this economic downturn sway their sales efforts. In fact, they turned it into an opportunity. People began to eat at home more often, rather than dining out. Mando organised 'Kyae' (a traditional private savings and social gathering system); a certain number of women paid to organise a group of members. Mando provided 11 products for each of 10 members. Each member who received the product had 10 months to pay for it and the organiser would get one free. Mando guaranteed 100 per cent after-sales service, since Mando had a much weaker franchise system than other competitive home-appliance giants such as LG (former Goldstar), Samsung and Daewoo. Mando supplied their products through department stores and home shopping channels. The marketing activities adopted by Mando proved to be very successful as they sold 180,000 units in 1998, an increase of 220 per cent over the preceding year. This was even more significant given that this growth occurred during an overall economic recession in Korea. This tremendous growth could only continue for the first few years until the big competitors came into the market. As expected, Mando's success stimulated major home-appliance companies to jump into the *Kimchi* refrigerators market. Samsung entered the market in 1998, and LG and Daewoo entered in 1999 and 2000 respectively, making this market highly competitive.

David in front of the Goliaths

Table 6.6 shows that, in terms of company size, Mando is no more than a pygmy when compared with LG or Samsung. LG and Samsung

Table 6.6	Company size comparison (2001)		
	Mando	LG Electronics	Samsung Electronics
Sales (billion Won)	883	16,601	32,380
Employees	1,751	32,000	44,000
Capital (billion Won)	142	1,031	19,474

Source: From each company brochure.

Table 6.7 Mando's sales volume and market share						
Year	1996	1997	1998	1999	2000	2001
Sales volume ('000s)	20	78	180	350	480	650
Market share (%)	90	85	66	55	55	54

Sources: Mando Company Brochure (2002) and market data.

Electronics were the major companies in this sector, occupying more than 90 per cent of the domestic home-appliance market, and some white goods market segments even have world class competition. These companies joining the *Kimchi* refrigerator market were the biggest challenge for Mando, though Mando had reinforced its financial position and has been able to upgrade its facilities due to investment by UBS Capital Consortium. One area of concern for Mando was that it had only 180 nation-wide franchises compared to over 1,500 each for its major competitors. Mando's market share had been declining from 90 per cent in 1996 to 55 per cent in 2000 (see Table 6.7) as major competitors entered the market. However, the rapid growth in the market meant that Mando's sales volume was still growing and they were able to maintain overall market leadership.

LG and Samsung are each aiming to gain market leadership of this segment by 2003. However, in spite of this market pressure and saturation, Mando is concentrating all of its efforts on holding the leading position in the market, since it created the market and still has the highest quality product. The company has a 90 per cent level of user satisfaction against a 65 per cent level for their competitors. They were chosen as the 'top product' in 1997 and received the 'best marketing' award in 2000. They continue to invest 5 per cent of sales into R&D; they founded the *Kimchi* Research Centre; and they developed the export market for Korean immigrants. They continue to be innovative and ahead of the major competition with the implementation of a comprehensive marketing plan, as shown in Table 6.8.

Mando's success story was not merely a lesson in positioning, as advocated by Ries and Trout (1979), but shows how consumer marketing really works. It also shows how a smaller company that understands the consumer can move quickly, and if it continues to innovate and create markets or market segments it can compete with much larger competitors. Perhaps by virtue of necessity, but closely allied to its inter-relationship with customers and consumers at every stage,

Table 6.8   Mando's marketing mix strategy

Product	Price	Place	Promotion
■ best quality ■ best taste ■ value-added function	■ seasonal difference ■ highest price	■ diversifying ■ specialised store ■ alliance with home shopping	■ *Kimchi* reference-maker ■ specialised image ■ event marketing ■ 'Kyae' promotion ■ members get members' promotion

Source: Mando Company Brochure (2002).

Mando clearly illustrates the difference between the rhetoric of marketing and its real application, with very positive results.

Summary and conclusion

The air we breathe consists of oxygen, nitrogen *and advertising*! We understand that. We also understand that marketing may be like a tree that grows differently depending on where it is planted. Thus, the concept and definition of rhetorical and real marketing might be different depending upon the location from which cases are derived. There may be a consensus of understanding in one country, but it might be very different in other countries, just as 'Zen' is understood differently by those in the East compared with those in the West.

Here we have shown how the concept of marketing was introduced academically and adapted practically. In many other underdeveloped countries, entrepreneurs may have an understanding or have ideas about marketing, but they are not necessarily free in their regimes and may encounter difficulties getting a consensus among the people that count. For Goldstar, it took decades to see the real marketing picture even though they had a very entrepreneurial start to their business. At the same time it might have been much easier for Mando to practise real marketing given that the business and marketing environment had improved in the late 1990s.

In summary, though we could not literally show it, we see differences between proclaimed marketing rhetoric and actual allegiance to it. Customer needs and wants do not have to be considered seriously in monopoly markets presided over by a dictatorship type of government. One difference between rhetoric and real marketing is that the latter no doubt works more efficiently when there is less time and fewer resources. Another difference lies in the way in which employees internally share core marketing beliefs and how much the market condition provides for free competition. In many cases, therefore, the difference between rhetoric and reality in marketing may depend as much on the socio-cultural context of a situation as on the strategies or concepts adopted by management.

The rhetoric and reality of marketing in Malaysia

7

rosmimah mohd-roslin

Aims

This chapter aims to:

- provide a glimpse of the business environment and examples of marketing reality and rhetoric practice in Malaysian businesses
- address current issues in these practices in the Malaysian business environment
- assess how customer satisfaction might be achieved through marketing strategies developed by two different businesses in Malaysia
- evaluate existing gaps between strategic plans and actual practice as seen in these two organisations

Overview

The importance of delivering customer satisfaction has always been at the core of marketing practice. Being able to provide customers with what they want and need conjures up the image of the effective marketer who is always ready to meet customer demands. In Malaysia, as with many other countries in the world, the continuity of businesses depends to a large extent on how well relationships are maintained and managed, not only with end-users but also with customers within the supply and distribution chain. To stay ahead, such relationships have to be groomed and nurtured so that continuity of the business is ensured.

Essentially, the weakness of many Malaysian corporations as regards handling customer relationship programmes effectively is well highlighted (Raghavan, 2002). The two cases discussed here serve to illustrate real examples of Malaysian businesses assessing customer needs and developing related strategies to meet these needs. The contrast between a service organisation that understands the importance of keeping track of changing customer wants, and a service industry that has long enjoyed widespread consumer dependence on their services, as depicted in the two cases, serves to highlight the differences in strategic orientation and marketing rhetoric and reality within the Malaysian business environment.

Marketing in Malaysia

Lasserre and Schutte (1999) assert that the Asia-Pacific region is one of those areas of the world where building and cultivating relationships are crucial to business development. Personal and reciprocal relationships are valued over mere contracts and transactions and this is often extended to customers at all levels of the business. However, in Malaysian firms, formal customer relationship programmes developed to meet customers' needs precisely have yet to be fully implemented and realised in effective practice. Inasmuch as personal relationships are regarded as prerequisites for many business relationships in the supply chain, this form of relationship has not yet been extended to include ultimate consumers. It is difficult at times to find business firms seriously practising and implementing formal relationship marketing programmes or developing some form of customer relationship management (CRM) efforts.

Nevertheless, the marketing concept is without question a well-understood principle among many Malaysian business firms. The realisation that customers are important and that marketing plans should centre on the needs of the customers is well documented and accepted, yet to what extent this is translated into meaningful applications is open to question, and perhaps even criticism. Many marketing writers have indicated a lack of sensitivity among Malaysian businesses as to the exact needs of their customers. Research on customer needs is almost unheard of in many businesses, especially among small and medium sized enterprises where resources for research are rarely a priority. It is therefore sensible to assess two cases, one in an industry that has become very competitive and saturated, and the other a service industry that may have become too complacent and have taken for granted the needs of customers. In both cases, the main aim of the discussion is to evaluate how effective marketing strategies are formulated and translated into applicable solutions, by using the rhetoric and reality construct.

Case 1: the Impiana Hotel, Kuala Lumpur

Opened in 1999, the Impiana Hotel joined the string of hotels offering a multitude of services for both local and international tourists visiting Kuala Lumpur, the capital city of Malaysia. The hotel is managed by Betaplan, which is owned by the Urban Development Authority (UDA) Holdings with a 51 per cent stake in the business, and the CAPP Group, a multinational resort operator in the region, which has a 49 per cent share. As a new entrant in the already saturated hotel industry, the management of the Impiana realised the importance of making its mark when introducing the hotel. The challenge was to develop a marketing blitz capable of turning heads during the initial launch of the hotel.

The General Manager of the Impiana Hotel, Syed Nazri, recalled how the management team contemplated the opening of the hotel in 1999. Even before the building was completed, the team sat countless times in front of the construction site discussing how the hotel was going to be positioned. Realising that the hotel was initially planned as a three-star hotel on the basis that there would be no swimming pool, the team visualised ways and means to attract the market. The first step was to look at what could be a competitive edge for the Impiana. Assessing the surroundings, Nazri saw the location as a plus point for the hotel. Located within walking distance of Chinatown, Malaysia's very own shopping haven for bargain hunters, Nazri realised that this could very well be the Impiana's selling point. In addition, the Impiana is also within walking distance of numerous other interesting spots such as the Central Market, Kuala Lumpur's cultural centre, *Dataran Merdeka* (Independence Square), and it is also easily accessible via the Light Rail Transit (LRT), and near the Puduraya Bus Station which serves as the transportation hub linking Kuala Lumpur with other states in the country.

Figure 7.1 Impiana Hotel, Kuala Lumpur

Creating the right positioning strategy appeared to be the main focus of management in the early stages. With a three-star image, the thought of positioning the hotel as yet another 'budget hotel' did not appeal to the management team. The hotel was more than the normal three-star budget hotel catering to the needs of local tourists in transit in the capital city or foreign tourists looking for cheap accommodation. Nazri saw that, upon completion, the hotel façade boasted a grand appearance, matched internally with polished marble flooring and exclusive furnishings. The three-star hotel with the four-star appearance prompted the management team to use this to their advantage in their early promotional efforts.

Nazri's motto was to 'create as much noise as possible'. This was indeed necessary to ensure that people were not only aware of the existence of the hotel but were ready to try it out. Whenever there was an opportunity to display the hotel to prospective customers, Nazri and his team were ever willing to comply. At an early stage, the hotel was involved in various marketing and promotional programmes that were meant to introduce the hotel and create awareness in the public. Public relations (PR) efforts were also high on the promotional agenda, as Nazri believed that PR represented the cheapest, yet the most effective, promotional tool. Press releases, via sponsorship of cultural and charity programmes, were among the projects carried out by the hotel.

Promotional efforts at an early stage of introduction proved to be quite successful and the Impiana was able to generate a 40 per cent occupancy rate within its first year of operation. Continuity of effort led to a 60 per cent occupancy rate in the second year, and the hotel targeted an 80 per cent occupancy rate in 2002. The formula for its continued success needs to be maintained, or even enhanced, but how this is to be done requires the management team constantly to assess new markets and identify their exact needs, a challenge which Nazri is willing to tackle.

In the initial phase, the Impiana was targeting tourists from China whose main attraction to Malaysia was (ironically) shopping and sight-seeing. Kuala Lumpur is indeed an attractive destination for the Chinese, who come as large tour groups organised by travel agents and who are then taken to various destinations in the country. The Impiana, therefore, tried to link up with the travel agents but eventually, as it was failing to meet the needs of both parties, this arrangement was terminated. The Impiana then moved on to focus on the Arab market, and the Singaporeans.

The Singaporeans have always been the largest group of tourists to Malaysia, contributing almost RM7.6 billion (approximately £1.4 billion) to Malaysian tourism revenue (Malaysia, 2001). It is therefore a lucrative market, which the Impiana is holding on to tightly. Essentially, tourists from ASEAN (Association of Southeast Asian Nations) countries represent the largest percentage of tourists visiting Malaysia, as indicated in Table 7.1. Tourists from the Middle East, however, are a relatively new market as the Arabs have only recently looked to Malaysia as a potentially attractive destination. Essentially, the 11 September 2001 tragedy has to some extent influenced this new outlook towards Malaysia as a possible destination among Arabs. The Impiana is now eyeing this potentially lucrative market as the Arabs are beginning to make their mark on the Malaysian tourist industry.

In 1998, tourists from the Middle East numbered only 23,854, but in 2001 this figure climbed to 114,776 (Malaysia, 2001). The amount of spending by tourists from the Middle East is estimated to be about RM376 million (approximately £70 million). In the year 2002, the

Table 7.1   Selected tourism indicators, 1995 and 2000

Indicator	1995	2000
Number of tourist arrivals ('000)	7,469	10,221
By country of origin (%)		
ASEAN[a]	73.5	70.3
Japan	4.4	4.5
China	1.4	4.2
Taiwan	3.9	2.1
Hong Kong	2.0	0.7
India	0.4	1.3
Australia	1.8	2.3
UK	2.2	2.3
USA	1.3	1.8
Others	9.1	10.5
Total tourism receipts[b] (RM million)	9,927.8	18,756.7
Number of hotels[c]	1,220	1,492
Number of hotel rooms	76,373	134,503
Average length of stay (nights)	4.8	5.5
Occupancy rate of hotel (%)	65.5	55.0
Employment[d]	67,214	78,671

[a] Excludes Myanmar, Vietnam and Cambodia
[b] Tourism receipts = tourist receipts + excursion receipts
[c] Hotels with 10 rooms and above, excluding service apartments and condominiums
[d] Employment covers the hotel industry only
Source: Eighth Malaysia Plan, 2001–2005.

Ministry of Arts, Tourism and Culture was targeting 250,000 Arab tourists to Malaysia. This is definitely an area which the Impiana cannot afford to ignore. Unlike Chinese tourists, however, the Arabs do not normally come in tour groups. Even if they do, the tour groups are usually small and consist of family members. Their preference for four- or five-star hotels is well noted and this represents a challenge to the Impiana in terms of developing effective strategies to woo them.

The constant change of focus on major target customers reflects the hotel industry where strategies have to be modified and altered to meet changing demands of different markets. Situational and environmental factors contribute to the fluctuations of tourist arrival in a country.

Nazri believes that the key to effective strategies is to know the customers very well, and within the hotel business this has to be done speedily and continuously. To some extent it is business instincts that dictate the course of action and the relevant applications in ensuring the continuous success of the hotel.

Being customer-centred means delivering exactly what customers want via superior value to customers. This seems to imply that all the staff in the Impiana need to be constantly alert to the changes that come with changing marketing strategies. In reality, although the Impiana realises the importance of formulating firm strategic guides in its marketing applications, the current scenario dictates actual market implementations. Changes in tourism patterns since its inception have forced the hotel to re-align its strategies with changing needs. Understanding that, in the hotel industry, customer needs differ among different sets of patrons often requires the Impiana to deviate from specified marketing plans. 'Know your customers!' is how Nazri describes the Impiana's guiding principle. The change in focus from the Chinese market to the Arabs and also to the Singaporeans meant that the management team had to be flexible in their strategic outlook to allow them to create appropriate marketing themes whenever the need arises.

This is often a challenging pursuit, as the Marketing Director, Shukri Yusof, accepts. Being able to keep pace with changing needs of customers is a must for those in this competitive industry. The hotel's three-star ranking has not helped much in enhancing the image of the hotel when competition from numerous four- and five-star hotels is ever-present. Yet the positive performance of the Impiana over its first three years has been impressive enough to warrant a positive outlook for the future. The stakeholders in the Impiana are confident that this little hotel will continue to do well if the sensitivity to changing customers and their needs is realised and implemented effectively by all levels of personnel in the hotel.

Nazri believes that another factor contributing to the Impiana's success in the past two years has been managerial efforts in employing personnel who add value to the hotel. The Impiana is especially proud of their key chefs who are hand-picked and are well taken care of by the hotel. Employees are always an asset which a hotel simply cannot neglect. This value-adding focus extends to customers since services provided by the staff are reflections of the hotel's capability. Put together, this may well be a recipe for success.

Case 2: banking services in Malaysia

The economic crisis of 1997 in south-east Asia severely jolted the financial scenario in the Pacific Rim region. What started as a financial crisis when currencies were devalued in Thailand, Malaysia, Indonesia, the Philippines and then South Korea later became an unprecedented economic crisis. The 'Asian miracle' of the 1980s turned into an 'Asian nightmare' in 1997, and sceptics were quick to comment on the downfall of the dragons of Asia. In retrospect, the crisis brought with it countless lessons, from improving transparency to greater market competence.

In Malaysia, after the severity of the crisis eased, Bank Negara, the country's central bank, responded with a close scrutiny of the banking industry. Figure 7.2 indicates the financial system structure in Malaysia. The need to compete effectively with foreign banks in the country as well as at the international level prompted the central bank to consider merging the 54 local commercial banks in the country into ten relatively strong banks. Putting their resources together, the ten merged financial institutions are more likely to strengthen their positions against other, more established and stronger foreign banks, and it is envisaged that they will be more able to face globalisation in the region.

The ten key commercial banking groups include Malayan Banking or Maybank, Bumiputera-Commerce Bank, RHB Bank, Public Bank, Hong Leong Bank, Alliance Bank, Perwira Affin Bank, Southern Bank and Eon Bank. Like it or not, changes are inevitable in the Malaysian banking sector and these ten banks are saddled with more responsibilities in ensuring competitiveness. Like many other financial sectors in developing nations, the banking industry in Malaysia is closely regulated, and without doubt has been subjected to stringent rulings and requirements. Yet a firm business orientation should still be of primary concern, and addressing consumer satisfaction must still be a priority.

In Malaysia, the banking industry has reached a point where employment layoffs and redundancies are widespread, and the banks' personnel are often forced to consider voluntary separation schemes (VSS). Despite the positive average growth rates of the total assets, total deposits and total loans of these financial institutions from 1995 until 2000, as indicated in Table 7.2, competition from foreign banks has become more apparent and there is now a dire need to identify

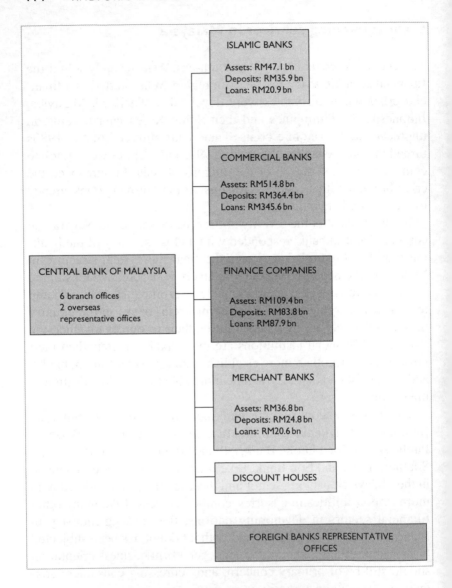

ISLAMIC BANKS

Assets: RM47.1 bn
Deposits: RM35.9 bn
Loans: RM20.9 bn

COMMERCIAL BANKS

Assets: RM514.8 bn
Deposits: RM364.4 bn
Loans: RM345.6 bn

CENTRAL BANK OF MALAYSIA

6 branch offices
2 overseas
representative offices

FINANCE COMPANIES

Assets: RM109.4 bn
Deposits: RM83.8 bn
Loans: RM87.9 bn

MERCHANT BANKS

Assets: RM36.8 bn
Deposits: RM24.8 bn
Loans: RM20.6 bn

DISCOUNT HOUSES

FOREIGN BANKS REPRESENTATIVE OFFICES

Figure 7.2   The Malaysian financial system structure: banking
institutions as at 31 December 2001

effective ways of competing effectively. In addition, the mergers are
not without extensive cost. Maybank, the largest banking group in
Malaysia, notes that in the fourth quarter ended 30 June 2000 it registered a net loss of RM29.375 million (approximately £5.4 million), as

Table 7.2 Average annual growth rates, 1996–2000 of total assets, deposits and loans in the banking system

Total assets		Total deposits	Total outstanding loans
Institutions	Average annual growth rate (%)	Average annual growth rate (%)	Average annual growth rate (%)
Commercial banks	11.7	13.1	13.7
Finance companies	3.5	3.7	6.3
Merchant banks	6.4	9.0	7.9

Source: Eighth Malaysia Plan 2001–2005.

against a net profit of RM345.74 million (approximately £64 million) a year earlier. This resulted in the group's full-year profit falling by 38 per cent from the previous year (Hanim, 2001).

At the consumer level, the mergers were greeted with mixed reactions. On the one hand, consumers believed that such mergers were likely to upgrade services since the pooling of resources meant that the ten banks had become stronger. On the other hand, some customers felt that personalisation of banking services would no longer be possible since large size is associated with distant and impersonal service.

Customer relationships have thus become an area of interest in the retail banking sector with banks becoming larger. Efforts towards upgrading banking operations have increased and the mergers have further enhanced the need to ensure that customer services are not only maintained but also improved, to ensure the continuity of customer patronage. The challenge of ensuring customer retention has prompted a number of new services to be introduced. Maybank, for instance, has been focusing on its priority banking services where customers with large accounts are given special privileges when carrying out their banking transactions.

The ten leading banks in Malaysia are indeed large enough to understand the importance of addressing customer needs. Millions of Malaysian ringgit have been spent on product development and promotional strategies to introduce modern banking services and facilities. Internet banking, for example, has caught the eye of many banks in the country and services including account enquiries, account transfers, bill payments, cheque status and trading of shares are among those offered. To a large extent, many of these new services are still not widely utilised by the masses despite the huge investments made by banks. A survey carried out by Mastercard in the Asian region revealed that three out of four Asian bank customers prefer to go into branches to deal with accounts rather than use Internet banking (*The Star*, 2001). Eighty-six per cent of Malaysian customers surveyed prefer the personal touch.

Promotional campaigns by many of the banks emphasise services offered, the benefits of their products, and how attractive their rates are. However, what is often missing in the banking services is that personal touch which most customers seek when stepping into the banks. Many of the banks in Malaysia are still holding on to the product concept where their services and offerings are highlighted in their promotional strategies as being of high quality, high value and most innovative. The missing link in many banks, however, is a focus on what customers really expect from service-oriented organisations. Enter any of the banks in the country and you will discover how impersonal and mechanical some banking personnel are. The front-liners who are bogged down by heavy workloads and routine operations rarely have time to smile at customers, let alone to get to know them. Yip Jian Lee, former director of the Institute of Banks Malaysia, feels that good customer relationships are a crucial ingredient that will ensure customer retention (Fong, 2000), yet this appears to be largely missing in the banking sector.

There is no question that the rhetoric of marketing stresses that effective marketing programmes go a long way towards enhancing business, and this is well documented in many of the banks in Malaysia through their marketing strategies. Recognising that promotion plays an important role, the banks are not reluctant to spend for such a purpose but, when an assessment of their promotional materials is made, one is able to see that a focus on building customer relationships is still noticeable by its absence. The extent to which tactical marketing plans are translated into effective customer relationship building has yet to be realised in many banks. At the front end, where customers are not made to feel welcome as queues are often long and depressing, the banks need to look long and hard at their service offering. Although technology has played a major role in improving many of the banking services, this effort still lacks comprehensiveness and unity. Much needs to be done to improve customer services and enhance customer relationships. Until that happens, all that marketing can be – in this particular sector – is just a form of words, pleasant and Western-sounding perhaps, but with no real accompanying commitment to analysing customer needs and then delivering the desired satisfaction.

The consolidation of the banking sector brings with it the challenge of merging different operational systems in the various banks, but this is not the greatest challenge. The toughest challenge, according to some analysts, is to ensure customer retention and to identify clearly what they can really sell to new customers, how to maintain existing customers, and what existing and new customers actually want (Sidhu, 2001). Another related factor that should be given due consideration is that of corporate culture. The mergers need to address the implications of differing corporate cultures and how these are translated into building relevant marketing programmes capable of meeting enhanced customer needs.

Perhaps the mergers have created a gap in assessing CRM, which bankers now have to address. Customers, according to Kotler and Armstrong (1996), are value maximisers. As customers are exposed to more information, banks have to consider how their value delivery system can and should be upgraded. CRM is but one aspect of relationship building that should be given more emphasis as competition becomes more pronounced. The intention of Bank Negara, Malaysia's central bank, to enhance the competitiveness of domestic banks despite globalisation and liberalisation of trade should indicate the importance of addressing ways of enhancing competitiveness and, to do this, the answer may well lie in how well the banks organise to meet customer requirements.

The rhetoric and reality of marketing: a review

The two cases derived from different service industries in Malaysia exemplify the importance of adhering to meticulous planning in marketing based on a sound understanding of the dynamics of served markets. In the case of the Impiana, plans have to change frequently and flexibility in meeting changing customer needs is paramount if a service organisation in a highly competitive industry (such as the hotel industry) is to survive in the long run. Plans that are developed at an early stage often have to be modified and, more often than not, the instincts of key decision-makers in the service organisations are crucial when deciding what should or should not proceed. Those in the hotel industry know only too well how plans can change when unprecedented situations arise. The marketing concept of clearly meeting the wants and needs of changing target markets is delivered by service organisations such as the Impiana, whose survival is dependent on how well it is able to meet customer requirements. Clearly, the Impiana has a developed and sophisticated view of marketing that extends beyond rhetoric to what has been termed elsewhere in this text as 'the reality of marketing'. The management team's realisation of how important it is to include the essence of marketing in all decision-making exemplifies the marketing reality.

On the other hand, the banking industry in Malaysia, which has undergone massive structural changes, is still adhering to the old ways of focusing on the product concept whilst focus on customer services is often off-target. Rhetorically, the banks have succeeded in portraying their understanding of the marketing concept but this has not been translated effectively at the operational stage. Indeed, much needs to be done to ensure greater sensitivity towards customer satisfaction. Rhetoric alone will not suffice. Although the banks have openly proclaimed their allegiance to marketing and their orientation towards ensuring customer satisfaction, the end results are not reflective of this. Essentially, their strategies are lost within the trappings of marketing, where promotional tools are the only indicators of their efforts.

Raghavan (2002) notes that customer relationship management is not about enabling the company to *sell* but rather getting the customers to *buy*. Essentially, the preparation a business firm undertakes to ensure that customers' requirements are well understood, and the steps taken to achieve customer satisfaction, are both critical to the success of the business: 'It is engaging the customer in dialogue while armed with full knowledge of his history and current needs, in order to proposition products he didn't know he needed' (Raghavan, 2002, p.10), is how customer relationship management is described.

In developed nations, many business firms have gone through the lifecycle where competition has forced many firms to delve deeper into the needs of customers so as to be able to satisfy them effectively and efficiently. In many developing nations, such as Malaysia, however, this need has not been realised fully. Service orientation in many business firms is still lacking in customer focus because many service providers have yet to internalise this need completely, and also because lack of training among the service staff has resulted in a lackadaisical attitude towards upgrading customer services.

Conclusion

The widespread acceptance of the marketing concept is without doubt an indication of its benefits. Even though many business firms pledge adherence to the marketing concept, how it is translated into applicable solutions differs substantially. Satisfying the wants and needs of customers is definitely critical in ensuring the continuity of businesses, but the methods of executing marketing tasks are often different, and to some extent dependent on the environment in which the business firm is operating.

In reality, many business firms have yet to transform the principle behind the marketing concept into applicable real solutions so that both customers and the firms will be able to achieve their objectives. Many business firms in Malaysia, although realising the direction which effective marketing orientations will take, have yet to transform strategies into efforts which will meet exact consumer needs. The inevitability of globalisation may speed up efforts towards enhancing customer satisfaction somewhat but this requires investment in the necessary infrastructure. Service and sales processes need to be integrated, marketing processes need to be individualised and customer data warehouses have to be linked to all those involved in providing the services. It is hoped that with coordinated efforts, the focus on customer orientation will indeed become a reality; no longer will marketing be a mere concept that is understood but not fully internalised by all in the business.

The rhetoric and reality of marketing in Bulgaria

8

vesselin blagoev

Aims

After reading this chapter you will be able to:

- trace the development of the marketing concept in Bulgaria over the past two decades
- understand the implication of the main factors influencing the application of marketing in that country
- characterise the basic difficulties which prevent the use of some of the most important marketing functions by small and medium sized companies
- analyse the activities and possible outcomes of the activities of the particular companies in the specific situations described in the two cases

Introduction

Marketing is not a new word in Bulgaria. The word first appeared in a scholarly paper in the 1960s (Krastev, 1967), which is quite late compared to the development of the discipline in the USA and the UK. At that time, and until the beginning of the 1990s, Bulgaria was an active participant in international trade. Over 80 per cent of its GNP came from foreign trade operations. That led to intensive application of the concept in all industrial branches which were dependent on export and import operations. The state-owned and municipal companies, and even the cooperative ones, were forced to take certain measures to improve their managerial capacity in the direction of innovation and finding new export markets beyond the Council for Mutual Economic Assistance (COMECON) markets.

As a small country which lacks large reserves of natural resources, Bulgaria did not have any alternative to successful competition in the Western world or Third World markets – the main sources of much-needed hard currency – except via application of the marketing concept. This approach to markets was applied to the other COME-CON markets as well. In spite of the centrally planned and controlled foreign exchange between the COMECON countries, each one of them participated in hidden (yet stiff) competition with the other countries for the Russian market and for developing in advance the technologies and new products which could be used for a claim on specialisation in the common market. The rules of the game were based upon specialisation of each country in specific industries and products, which were then supplied to all COMECON countries. Based on active marketing and technical development, Bulgaria specialised in the production of mainframes, PCs and software, computer-machined tools, ships, fork lift trucks, hoists, electrical machines and equipment for energy generation, cigarettes, wine and liquors, textiles and garments, grain, fruits and vegetables (see Krastev, 1977). They were exported mainly to the COMECON countries, and about 10 per cent were exported to the West, Asia and Africa.

After the huge political changes at the start of the 1990s the COMECON market collapsed and the mass of exports to that destination had to be redirected to other markets. Simultaneously, this was accompanied by a period of active industrial disintegration. The 462 previously established vast state companies divided into many smaller companies, many of whom did not have the necessary expertise and experience in the fields of marketing and foreign trade. As a result, many industries, which were too big for the scale of Bulgaria, found themselves without any markets. The Bulgarian market was far too small to absorb what the production facilities could produce. It was not possible to increase the exports to the West, Middle East and Far East over five times to substitute for the COMECON markets which were lost (see Table 8.1). The transition period turned out to be disastrous for many industries and they simply disappeared from the export list (see Table A8.1 in the appendix).

Table 8.1	Bulgaria's foreign trade, 1990–93 (1990=100%)			
	1990 (%)	1991 (%)	1992 (%)	1993 (%)
Export	100	25.6	29.2	26.7
Import	100	17.6	34.0	32.9

They could not compete in the Western markets with products of the required quality, or services which could serve the consumers in those markets better. Many companies were in debt due to the huge investments made in the period of the increase of production facilities, which was supposed to serve the needs of the markets in the USSR. All these dynamic changes marked the rapid development of the marketing concept in the 1990s. Some of them happened probably because of the lack of use, or misinterpretation, of this concept by the industrial and market agents. This chapter gives us an opportunity to analyse and understand the specifics of the development of the discipline in all these years of transition.

Development of the marketing concept in Bulgaria

In the late 1970s the Bulgarian state issued a set of regulations aimed at increasing the competitiveness of Bulgarian companies in international markets. At that time Bulgarian industry comprised about 2,000 state-owned and about 1,000 municipal companies. By the end of the 1980s they were expected to merge into about 500 state-owned and 600 municipal companies, all of them having enough of their own weight and resources to compete successfully in international markets.

According to the same directives, by the early 1980s every Bulgarian company was supposed to have a marketing, or a marketing and sales, department. Foreign trade was concentrated in 84 foreign trade companies, which were obliged to survey the markets and serve producers with the full range of marketing activities, directed primarily to these international markets. There were branches of the industry for which Bulgaria was a world-class exporter in spite of its size. With a population of less than 9 million Bulgaria managed to develop the biggest producer of fork lift trucks in the world (each year

Balkancar plc produced about 58,000 fork lift trucks, plus about 30,000 industrial trucks and 117,000 electric hoists, which were exported to over 50 countries including Japan, the UK, France and Italy, among others). Bulgaria exported to Europe, Asia and Africa CNC machine tools, chemicals, electrical machines and equipment for energy generation, textile and garments, wine, tobacco, grain, fruits and other products. All these exports to Western Europe, the USA and elsewhere provided much-needed hard currency for the development of new plants and even gigantic projects such as the biggest and most modern factory for heavy equipment in Europe, which was built near Sofia, the biggest company for mainframes and PCs in East Europe, and other similar enterprises.

Thus, in the 1980s, Bulgaria was listed among the developed nations. As could be expected the export orientation of Bulgaria influenced the development and the implementation of the marketing concept. In the 1970s and 1980s most publications in the field were discussing marketing problems in foreign trade (see, e.g., Doganov and Radoicheva, 1984, 1987; Karakasheva and Boeva, 1979; Keremidchiev, 1975; Krastev, 1977; Maneva, 1984; Todorov, 1984). Even in papers discussing other marketing issues, such as product policy, the analysis was always export-oriented (Blagoev, 1984a,b). Some publications addressed marketing management problems (Blagoev, Kirkov and Milanova, 1986; Bozduganov et al., 1984; Kirkov and Blagoev, 1983). Publications on marketing problems connected with the local market were noticeably much fewer in number. The local or national market was always the weak point in terms of quality of products and services and consumer satisfaction (Doganov and Malamin, 1983; Vassilev et al., 1981).

The first textbook on marketing written by a Bulgarian author was published by Emil Keremidchiev (1975). However, his text was followed by Karakasheva and Boeva (1979); Vassilev et al. (1981); Bozduganov et al. (1984); Blagoev, Kirkov and Milanova (1986); Blagoev (1988); Keremidchiev (1990); and Marinova (1992). The first half of the 1990s was marked by a proliferation of translated textbooks from American, French, German and even Russian scholars. Interest in marketing and in implementation of the marketing concept was enormous. This could be illustrated by the fact that 30,000 copies of the first two editions of *Marketing in Definitions and Examples* (Blagoev, 1988, 1989) were sold in less than a month. Many felt that they could not solve the problems faced by their companies in any way other than marketing. The demand for marketing books and the interest of scholars led to many publications in the 1990s including textbooks such as Jelev (1995); Marinova (1996); Karakasheva, Mencheva and Markova (1997); Hristov (1998); Mladenova (1998); Doganov (1998); Blagoev (1998); and Klassova *et al.* (1999). By 2002 marketing programmes were offered at over 20 Bulgarian universities, and marketing units were taught in over 50 universities, including The International University, which offers programmes validated by the University of Portsmouth (UK).

The marketing concept and the companies

The necessity to export in order to earn much-needed hard currency led to relatively fast adoption of the marketing concept by foreign trade companies and by industrial companies. Based on the state directives they established marketing departments or marketing and sales departments, which were responsible for monitoring the foreign markets of interest and for planning all marketing activities, thus supporting market entry and exporting. Electroimpex plc, for example, had representative offices in over 20 countries. In Germany, France, Italy, Spain, Russia, Singapore and some other countries it had joint ventures with local partners, which carried out marketing activities along with sales and technical support of its products. Through such joint ventures and offices, operating in the main export markets, Electroimpex was in a position to conduct marketing surveys and plan a relatively wide range of other marketing activities which were specific to most of the markets.

The marketing planning process usually started in July. Based on the analysis of sales data by markets and on available information about development of these markets, the marketing department sent questionnaires to all representatives asking for additional information and early forecasts for the next year. Special attention was paid to markets where new tenders for supply of equipment or turnkey projects were expected in the next year. For every market of interest the marketing department prepared market profiles, which were updated two to three times each year. In April each year the marketing department and the advertising department worked out a proposal for participation in the international trade fairs and exhibitions during the next planning year, as well as proposals for special promotions and exhibitions which were organised by Electroimpex in some of the markets (depending on the marketing plan). Based on the analysis of the market surveys and on other available information every year the marketing department prepared a marketing programme, or market and pricing policy, which was then presented for approval to the Board of Directors and the Ministry of Foreign Trade. All managing directors of the production companies, which had shares in Electroimpex plc and which exported and imported through it, were members of its Board of Directors. These procedures led to relatively good coordination of marketing activities in the foreign trade and production companies in all the markets of interest.

Marketing systems for the local market were organised differently. Every shop, manager or shift manager in the shop was responsible for entering consumers' questions and requests in a notebook. Department stores had different notebooks in each department. These notebooks were considered to be a very important source of market information, along with the store order forms. Depending upon the product line, the companies had different systems for further coordination of the marketing activities. The garment industry, for example, had two special fairs for contracting their collections one year ahead. Most of these companies produced mainly export products. They were interested in adding new orders to the orders for collections already contracted for export to France, Germany, Canada, Benelux, the Czech Republic, and so on. However, they were supposed to present all their collections to these special fairs and offer them to the representatives of the regional wholesale companies. In reality, many of the products ordered for export found hardly any customers among those representatives, although theoretically the wholesalers were expected to act in the most reasonable way from the point of view of the market. Ironically, very often the representatives of the wholesalers ordered goods which differed a great deal from what was chosen by the international distributors. Thus a potential marketing system for surveying the market (with the aim of customer servicing) degenerated as a result of faulty implementation.

One of the most important factors for the implementation of marketing were regulations about the innovation process. According to that regulation every company was supposed to launch at least 3 per cent of their total product line as new products in the market each year. The amount of sales of those new products was supposed to contribute at least 5 per cent of the annual sales if the management of the company were to receive bonuses. On the other hand, consumers were protected in terms of the quality of products and services, so that all new products in the market had to be well engineered and tested.

As can be seen (at least theoretically) there was an established and relatively well-balanced system for development and implementation of the marketing concept. However, in spite of all these regulations and ostensible marketing activities Bulgaria still had a deficient economic system. The misinterpretation of the strategic goals of the economy and the disproportionately strong development of the production of tools and equipment compared to consumer goods led to constant deficits of different products. A deficit always discredits the system of regulations, leading to misinterpretation or ignorance of the system (the marketing concept in our case). Thus Bulgaria experienced a relatively well-developed system of marketing regulations and evident managerial strong interest for the discipline, combined with misinterpretation and ignorance of even basic principles of the marketing concept. As a result many companies developed export strategies and also general strategies so as to profit from the existing deficits. In 1985, for example, I was surprised to find a company exporting to the USSR the same agricultural machine it had been exporting without any change whatsoever for 17 years. Their excuse for the lack of innovation was that they offered the market a product which obviously satisfied their consumers. It is clear, however, that such marketing and innovation laziness does not contribute to the quality of life and could never be successful in a non-deficit economy.

The contemporary situation in the field of marketing

Bulgaria is still going through a transition period. After the massive privatisation processes that took place between 1994 and 2000 there are now very few natural monopolies, such as the telecommunication company, railways, major electric power generation facilities, and the ports and airports, which are planned for privatisation in 2002–3. Over 5,000 companies have been privatised and theoretically they are run just as every other company in the free market economy. In addition to this quite a large number of private companies have been privatised by foreign investors, such as Nestlé, Coca-Cola, ABB, Interbrew, Solvay,

American Standard, and others. All major marketing channels of distribution exist and are actively used. These include, for instance, the classical channels of distribution and advertising and promotion channels, as well as Internet marketing options, e-commerce, and a wide spectrum of PR and promotion events. A good illustration of this is the fact that there are over 40 cable television channels, five of them national, in Bulgaria. An ordinary cable subscriber receives between 40 and 80 local and foreign television programmes, including CNN, BBC World Service, EuroNews, DW, ZDF, DSF, TV5, Rai Uno, RTP, National Geographic, M6, TG2, RTL, RTL 2, TCM, MUZZIK, HALLMARK, SAT 1, VOX, Sky Sports, Eurosport and others.

Every day a national channel, Channel 1, shows over 60 minutes of teleshopping in blocks of 15 minutes, in addition to over a hundred other commercials in 2–3 minute blocks. The other four national television channels have similar amounts of advertising content. The national, regional and local cable television channels show as many commercials as they can get from the vendors. Over 90 national, regional and local radio stations broadcast hundreds of commercials each day. Sofia – the capital of Bulgaria – and all other major towns are full of posters and billboards. Many international and local companies promote aggressively. An example of such aggressive promotion is the case of Kamenitsa Brewery (it is a part of Interbrew, Belgium, which is the fourth-largest brewery in the world). In 2000 Kamenitsa organised a lottery with a prize of a flight to Paris with a ticket for the European football championship. Every person who could present five labels from Kamenitsa beer participated in the lottery. Brewinvest (Greece) offered a Peugeot car and many PCs, audio systems and other prizes to participants in their contest. Many other companies from different industrial sectors also organise lotteries, games, contests, and so on. After several cases of penalising the organisers of such promotions (because of the expensive prizes compared to the price of the product), the organisers began to request applications only for the biggest prizes, while for every smaller prize, such as television sets, they still required labels, empty packs, and so on to be presented by participants in the contest or lottery. Altogether these examples show that the range of marketing methods, tools and options used in Bulgaria is quite similar to what can be seen in every Western market. It is important also that Bulgaria is a member of the World Trade Organisation and that there are no restrictions or regulations which differ from those in the UK or in the EU in general.

Marketing mimics

Theoretically all the factors described above must surely guarantee a well understood and well implemented marketing concept in Bulgaria? The reality, however, tends to deviate from what the theory may suggest. The major differences are found in the application of the following marketing elements:

- marketing research
- segmenting the markets
- market tests
- implementation of marketing in the R&D process

The lack of substantial marketing research characterises the implementation of marketing in almost all companies. There are two major reasons for this: lack of available statistical information at the micro level and lack of financial resources, which the companies need to pay for or to carry out market and marketing surveys using company structures for the field research. Case 1 illustrates this problem with regard to the new product development.

Similar problems are visible in the fact that most of the companies do not segment their markets of interest, and neither do they recognise the need for such segmentation. Sales forecasts, for example, are often made on the basis of irrelevant or aged market information. Using, for example, ACORN (a classification of residential neighbourhoods) or any other socio-demographic system is unheard of in Bulgaria. The fact is that many businesses operate on a follow-my-leader basis, thus running much higher risks when they start or develop their businesses, compared to what they theoretically would accept if they knew the market and the competitors better.

Another factor is the cultural specifics, which with some irony one could call 'market bravery based on marketing blindness'. Quite a few new private owners and managers believe that what the theory suggests 'will not happen to them'.

Market tests are not applied in many cases for different reasons. For many products the size of the country makes it difficult to plan for markets smaller than the national. Thus companies often rely on follow-my-leader strategies as regards innovation, advertising, sales and other elements of the marketing mix. The higher risk is not taken into account: 'If the leaders are doing it, why shouldn't we?'

The last problem of misinterpretation of the marketing concept is related to the application of marketing in the innovation process. It is a serious issue because it leads to two major risks:

- development of products which are not competitive enough or for which demand is insufficient
- customers' dissatisfaction, which ruins the image and the market position of the company

Case 2 illustrates the extensive use of marketing by the SPARKY Group, a major producer and exporter of electric hand-tools from Bulgaria to over four dozen markets in Europe, Asia and Africa. In this case the company has applied the marketing concept with a full understanding of the importance of satisfying the customer's needs and requirements better than the competitors so as to defend and further maintain the image of a world-class producer and exporter.

Case 1: the rhetoric of marketing and the case of the Pink Wafer

The Wafer-4 team members entered the Board of Directors meeting room with mixed feelings. It was great that things finally had come to the point when the decision about whether to go on with the project or kill it would be made. On the other hand, so much was at stake with the launch of this new and potentially successful product that team members probably would not mind having a few more days to crunch the numbers. But they were pressed for time and their preferences did not matter. The meeting room was already full of Board members and a few colleagues from the marketing department who were discussing the previous item on the Board's agenda. George Peev, the Head of the Wafer-4 team, pointed to the screen and said, 'I'll go there and set up the laptop. Mike and Ann – sit next to me, please. Tony, be ready to give the new handouts to the Board members.'

Stavros Nivolaou, CEO of Sofia Sweets plc, waved to George inviting him to take a seat next to the screen, and looked around to make sure that everybody was prepared to concentrate on the new topic. Nivolaou had been nominated CEO after the privatisation of the company, which had taken place a couple of years earlier. Until then Sofia Sweets had been one of the 15 state-owned companies, established 28 years earlier, which had been known for its biscuits and chocolate products. There were three products which had deservedly won for Sofia Sweets the image of a market leader in the field. The consumers voted every day on the image of the company through their preferences, and their favourites were its Sun Wafer, Mixed Chocolate bonbons and Sweet Pinocchio. These three products accounted for over 46 per cent of the sales and over 80 per cent of the profit of Sofia Sweets from 1990 to 1999. Thanks to them the company was able to experiment with new products every year, most of which had never reached break-even point. However, in the years before 1990 they did enable the company to increase the number of new products by 5 per cent each year. That was a state requirement if management and staff wanted to receive extra bonus payments at the end of every quarter. After 1990 these 5 per cent of new products per annum were no longer a state-controlled parameter, but designers and management nevertheless continued to develop and introduce new products to the market so as 'to fulfil the obligations'. When Stavros Nivolaou took over the CEO position, he was absolutely amazed to discover that one of his main tasks – to develop a spirit of market-driven innovation in the company – did not seem at all difficult to achieve, as marketing had already existed for at least a decade.

Stavros opened the meeting: 'Let us start with the second point in our itinerary for today. As everybody knows, with our wafers we have come to the point when we must decide whether to launch a new product and discontinue the old one or just stop producing the old wafer and forget about this market niche, which accounted for 17% to 25% of our sales and profit a year ago, and almost twice that just a decade ago. I must say that in my professional career I have never seen such market development. In just a year, consumer preferences have changed so much that after being in the position of market leader, we have ended up where we must fight just to keep our name in the market. I have never seen a market where consumer preferences change so fast. We must have been blind-sided by the previous success of the old wafer. We failed to notice either what the competitors were doing in terms of new products or in their aggressive marketing campaigns. Let me remind everybody here that we must either find a way to launch a successful new product on to the market, or we simply forget about this ex-cash cow, which Sofia Sweets was milking for so many years. George, you now have the floor. Please make good use of your time. We are big boys with broad shoulders here and we do not need fancy words but meaningful proposals.'

George Peev replied: 'Thank you Mr Nivolaou. Ladies and gentlemen, as you know our Wafer-4 group was formed to work on a project for a new wafer, which should replace our Sun Wafer. The team members are Mike Petrov, our chief technologist, who has worked on most of our wafers in the last decade; Ann

Ivanova from the Marketing Department; and Tony Tonev from our Innovation Department. I am head of that department, as you know.'

Stavros: 'George, come to the point please. The team was formed by decision of this Board, so I presume that all of us here know who's who in the team.'

George: 'I only wanted to underline that we wanted to have some of our best people in the team because we know how important this task is. Now, we have done a lot of work in the last six months and the results have been presented to you in the files which all of you have in front of you already. I'll summarise things as they have appeared after our research. First, we found out that the consumer perception of our current wafer has changed from "No. 1 – My first choice" to "No. 4 – I never think of it". I am referring to the results from the marketing survey. The reason for that seems to be the extensive introduction of new wafer type products by the competion, in much nicer packaging than ours. In terms of taste, the findings of the marketing people are that consumers still remember with pleasure the taste of our wafer. But they also say that they like the new taste of the competition's products. You can see all this in the survey results. So, based on these marketing findings, we developed our new Wafer-4, which we present to you. Our opinion is it should be launched in the market as soon as possible. I won't bother you with other figures, suggestions or conclusions, but we would be glad to answer any questions.'

Stavros: 'Thanks, George. Now, are there any questions? Yes, Peter Stanev.'

Peter Stanev was a new member of the Board. He had been a university lecturer, and this ostensibly generates an ability to see things in the company management from a different point of view.

Peter: 'George, would you elaborate a bit on how you got the data about consumer preferences?'

George: 'As I said, we got these data from our marketing department and Ann will explain everything in detail if necessary. From what I know, we have used the same methodology since the early 1980s. We ask our distributors to fill in questionnaires with all sorts of questions and we check the results by interviewing two focus groups: one formed by 11 clients and one formed by 11 employees of Sofia Sweets who are considered experts on the matter. Ann can tell you more about how we select the numbers of the clients' focus group.'

Ann: 'Yes, we usually ask 11 kids from the school across the street to act as experts. The idea is that the wafer is primarily a product for kids. We meet them there, in the school, so that everything looks as close to the real market situation as possible.'

Stavros: 'Good. Other questions?'

Peter: 'I do not quite understand. How can we be sure that we are obtaining enough real market information – information about trends in the market – if we only talk to our own distributors, a few kids across the street and a few employees of our company? Out of the three mentioned I would hardly describe even one as being a source of really objective information. They all are dependent on us.'

Stavros: 'George?'

George: 'Well, not at all. Who else would be a source of objective information, but the distributors? They sell all the stuff, which is offered by us, and our competitors. So they can compare. And they are absolutely interested in providing objective information, because they profit from our sales. If we sell, so do they. If we offer a bad product, they do not sell either. So I would not say that we hold subjective information, even if our data mining were a bit different from what theory might suggest.'

Stavros: 'OK, George. How did you develop the new product? I mean, we have introduced over 10 new wafers in the last 4 years and none of them paid back even the investments.'

George: 'Well, we started with an analysis of the current situation in the market. We compared the products on sale and filled a table with their main characteristics. Then we assigned special tasks to all our team members: new taste, new packing, new label, new name, new font, everything. Just as an example, our technologists prepare different mixtures of cocoa and sugar and we fill a matrix with the findings when we taste the mixture.'

'So you prepare the mixtures and then you decide which mixture tastes better', Peter Stanev said with a tone of surprise in his voice.

George: 'Yes, of course. There is no other way and everybody in the wafer production business does it this way. We prepare mixtures with a 0.3% difference in the cocoa and sugar amounts. And we are absolutely objective in our findings, because we know that our company and our salaries depend upon our results.'

Stavros: 'We do not question your objectivity, George. I have seen this happen in our factory in Greece also. I still do not understand why the wafers shouldn't taste like our wafers in Greece, but that's a matter of national taste, I guess. I would always prefer the Greek taste, I suppose. Other questions?'

Peter: 'Why did you decide that the new packing has to be like the one proposed here? I can remember we discussed that this packing does not provide better protection and it is 18% more expensive as well. Why did you decide that it's better? And why pink? I would doubt that consumers would ever be excited about pink packaged wafers.'

George: 'The thing is that the competition developed a new perception about this packaging and we can't ignore it unless we double our advertising budget to overcome the current problems. It would be better to spend that money on a new machine for the new packing. It is unclear what we would have after an advertising campaign defending our traditional packing. But if we buy the new machine we will have identical packing and a machine which can be used for years. One shot, two rabbits. The colour is really strange, but the marketing people here say that all other flashing colours are already used by the competition. So, why not pink?'

Stavros: 'Well, I see you have done everything as before. Why, then, didn't you have successful products with your previous teams? Why are you so sure that this time you have developed 'the product'?'

George: 'It is hard to say. My personal feeling is that we never supported our new products with a strong marketing campaign before. Look what the competitors do – less tasty products, smaller in volume, but nicely packed and supported by strong and efficient marketing campaigns. And the consumers respond positively. I would say they respond even faster than I would expect.'

Stavros: 'Good; let us come to the conclusions and to the decision. Yes, Mrs Gorova?'

Mrs Gorova: 'I support Wafer-4. I like the taste and the packing seems to respond to market preferences. From what I see in the tables of the marketing survey we are going in the right direction. The sales forecasts seem to be good enough. I am in favour of Wafer-4.'

Peter: 'I do not know what to say. Everything here sounds like reality but I have the feeling that we are behaving like in a child's game. We play producers and we mix ingredients, then we play consumers and we like our own mixtures. Then we change hats again and we like "what the consumers like". I feel a bit lost. I even see, here in the proposal, a budget for "an intensive and efficient marketing campaign", but there is no plan, budget, or even an idea for such a campaign. I do not see what to vote for. To me this paper sounds like an assessment of a prototype, not a proposal for the launch of a new product. I may be, wrong of course.'

Stavros: 'Well, Peter is our academic devil's advocate here. We must always consider the words of academics, because they foresee the future. However, from what I know from my professional career this is the way to develop new products in our business and Sofia Sweets was so successful for decades as a result of such marketing-driven consistent work on new products. To cut it short, I shall vote for the Pink Wafer-4. Let us go ahead as fast as possible. It will take us at least four months to deliver the new packing machine and start the production, so there is enough time to work out the marketing plan as well. Are there other suggestions? No? OK. The Board has spoken. We will press ahead.'

No endorsement is needed for Case 1. It represents realistically the matters that transpired in a strategic business unit, now belonging to a multinational. The story and names have been disguised.

Case 2: the reality of marketing and the case of BPR 241E: product positioning

'Hello, Peter. We'll be in Sofia in about half an hour. Call the team and please be ready to report on 241E.' The announcement was expected, yet bothersome. Peter Atanassov was Managing Director of SPARKY Sofia, and also team leader of the project for the launch of the new rotary hammer known as BPR 241E. SPARKY Sofia had been responsible for the commercialisation of 241E, which was expected to be the new champion of SPARKY Group in the electric hand-tool field. Including the market tests, it had taken over two years to develop 241E. In March 2001 it was shown at the Cologne Fair, the biggest international forum for new electric hand-tools. At the time it was just a prototype of the new professional powerful rotary hammer. Dozens of business meetings with the SPARKY Group's sales companies around the globe and with many other independent intermediaries proved that the new product had a high potential for market success. SPARKY Russia, SPARKY UK and SPARKY South Africa, as well as SPARKY Iran, placed orders for 200 to 550 tools to test the market. In addition to this, Stanislav Petkov and Peter Babourkov (the CEOs of SPARKY Group) were able to convince 23 independent partners with dealership operations to test 241E in laboratories and/or in the markets in their countries. Most of the SPARKY sales companies would have gone for the 241E along with the others, but they still had unsold stock of BPR 241E and they did not want to take big risks with cash flow. 'You are dead, guys. The world already knows that we are launching the 241E', Nikolay Kalbov teased his partners. He was Managing Director of SPARKY Eltos, a production company in Lovech, Bulgaria, which had designed all SPARKY's new electric hand-tools except for the cordless models.

Kalbov was really happy with the reaction of the market. The International Fair in Cologne was the meeting point for several thousand of trading companies who came every year to see the new trends and the new models of electric hand-tools, presented by over 200 producers, including Bosch, Black & Decker, De Walt, Makita, and many others. SPARKY had deservedly won the reputation of being an internationally recognised producer of such equipment, of professional quality and at reasonable prices. Although some salespeople said that the reasonable prices were not the result of a smart marketing strategy, but merely a newcomer's attempt to find a place in the sun, the result was undoubtedly positive.

SPARKY Group had been selling Eltos electric hand-tools to Russia and about ten other markets, most of which had been part of the USSR, since 1993. The contract with the producer gave SPARKY Group the right to be a sole agent for the brand name in the specified territories, thus protecting its position as the biggest intermediary in these lands, but it gave certain advantages to Eltos Ltd as well. The brand name SPARKY first appeared on electric hand-tools in 1994. It was adopted for the strategic business unit in the market after the privatisation of Eltos Ltd, Lovech, by the SPARKY Group, which was finalised in October 1996. In 1995 Eltos doubled its exports to Russia, compared to 1993 when this partnership was established, without investing anything in marketing or sales. SPARKY took over the responsibility for marketing and selling the tools. When Eltos was offered for privatisation, SPARKY Group was forced to give up its comfortable position as a distributor of electric hand-tools who did not have to worry about the production problems. Still, it had to think about the protection of its investments in the commercialisation of these products. After a series of negotiations with the Agency for Privatisation in Bulgaria and with its bankers, SPARKY Group decided to go for vertical integration. Thus, electric hand-tools became one of its leading product groups along with metals, computer hardware, garden equipment and luxury shoes. Only three years after privatisation SPARKY had achieved the biggest market share among importers to the Russian market as well as to Ukraine and Kazakhstan. In 2001 SPARKY accounted for over 32 per cent of the imports of electric hand-tools in Russia.

Many management decisions had paved the way for these market results. Soon after privatisation, SPARKY Group took several strategic decisions directed at optimisation of the performance of its distribution network. SPARKY Sofia was made responsible for the coordination of the marketing and sales activities in Russia, Ukraine, Belarus, Kazakhstan, Iran, Iraq, Egypt, Syria, Macedonia, Poland, the Czech Republic, Romania, Hungary, the South African Republic, Tunisia and Italy. The Electric Hand-tools Department in Berlin was made responsible for marketing and sales in Germany, France, Benelux, Sweden, Norway and the UK. SPARKY Eltos (the production company, which replaced Eltos Ltd after the privatisation) was taking care of the production and sales in Bulgaria. Besides its other activities, SPARKY Sofia was responsible for global sales monitoring and reported weekly to the Group CEOs.

One of the important factors for the success of the new product was the artistic design of the new tools. In 1999 the Group decided to establish an Artistic Design Department as a part of SPARKY Sofia, which soon was able to design over 30 new products a year in close cooperation with the technical design and technology departments in SPARKY Eltos, Lovech. That became possible when all designers, both in Sofia and Lovech, were equipped with powerful computer-aided design (CAD) systems and, most importantly, when they started really to use these systems. With all these changes SPARKY Group was able to use its marketing, sales, design and production resources much more effectively to satisfy consumer preferences, which changed every year as a result of the stiff competition in every market. A very important step in this direction was the establishment of 23 service centres for after-sales service in the guarantee period and partnership agreements with over 200 service centres for the off-guarantee period. This enabled the Group to acquire precious information and ideas for improvement of existing products and development of new ones, which would definitely serve the customers better.

Apart from that, SPARKY Group decided to establish and launch its new brand name, SPARKY, in the electric hand-tools market. It took about a year before everyone in the management was convinced that the markets would accept the new brand name. The surveys showed no serious problems in the non-English speaking countries, although it was clear that some 5–7 per cent decline in the sales within a year might be expected before the consumers accepted the new brand name, which came with a new design. It was also clear that it was necessary to increase the advertising budget substantially. The most negative effect of all were the expected red figures in the cash flow and overall sales results because of the necessary discounts for the Eltos brand-name tools if SPARKY Group were to try to sell them off as fast as possible until the markets got used to the new brand name. Stanislav Petkov and Peter Babourkov knew perfectly well that if the old tools were not sold in a year they would probably be good only for the SPARKY Eltos museum. Once the consumers had accepted the new brand name associated with new tools, which were more powerful and with a much improved design, they would hardly buy 'old stuff', no matter what the price was. The managers of the SPARKY trading companies in the UK and the South African Republic reported that the connotation of the word 'sparky' was not unconditionally positive, as some people used it to describe a semi-qualified professional in the electric field. However it was presumed that over 95 per cent of the sales of SPARKY would come from non-Anglo-Saxon markets, where the consumers definitely associate the word with professional electrical jobs with a positive connotation. Based on this Petkov and Babourkov had approved the new brand name and the budget for launching it.

Peter Atanassov phoned the other key players in the 241E team and told them to be ready to report on the team's campaign proposal in 45 minutes. The team had been formed about three months earlier with the task of coordinating the activities of the Group concerning commercialisation of 241E in all the markets. To be more precise, the Group had done a lot of work on the commercialisation in the past 12 months, since the first presentation of the 241E prototype at the Cologne Fair. To some degree the current plans and programmes simply integrated the strategies of the Group into one consistent strategy, based on all the research, analysis and current improvements of the product according to the suggestions from the laboratory and the market tests, as well as from the after-sales service centres. In spite of the prevailing positive reactions from the distributors and the partners, SPARKY Eltos and SPARKY Sofia did a lot of work to make some changes in the prototype in accordance with the quality standards and market conditions in the main markets. Nikolay Kalbov and Peter Atanassov, who closely supervised the work done in the technical design, technology, production and the artistic design departments, had their daily briefings on the issue in addition to the Friday afternoon meetings, which summarised 'the two Ps of the week', progress and problems to deal with. They often admitted to each other their surprise that the last two years of market and laboratory testing of 241E had been more successful, in terms of real production and sales, than many other new product launches, which never paid back the initial investment. Nevertheless 241E continued to be developed strictly following the SPARKY rules for marketing and R&D, no matter what the sales results were. The CEOs of the group wanted a large-scale operation where nothing was left to chance. As a result the operations for the commercialisation were planned and controlled almost as if it was a military campaign for simultaneous launch in about 25 markets.

The door opened and the two CEOs of SPARKY Group entered, together with Nikolay Kalbov. They had been in Lovech for the Board of Directors meeting of the production company and used the travel time from Lovech to Sofia to continue the discussions on some of the issues on the agenda.

'Hi, Peter. How's life?', said Stanislav Petkov.

Then Peter Babourkov said: 'Happy to see you Peter. Is there anything important and urgent to be discussed before we start the meeting on 241E?'

Atanassov: 'Not really. You must have got the sales report for the month by now. Everything seems to be under control. Shall I call the people, or will you take a few minutes before we start?'

'Let us start. Where do we meet?'

'In the meeting hall. We are about 15 people.'

Atanassov asked the secretary to call the team into the meeting room and took his laptop to use with the multimedia projector in case he needed to show something. The meeting was not intended to present new findings. Everything of potential use during the discussion had already been printed and filed for everyone on the team and the two CEOs. However, experience showed that, no matter how well everything was prepared, some tables and figures from one survey or another often needed to be shown. Two minutes later the meeting room was full of people. Present were the Chief Designer of 241E, the Head of the Artistic Design Department, the Head of the Marketing Department, and also the three special consultants of the Group's CEOs.

About a dozen of the SPARKY Group's country managers were asked to be available in their offices in Moscow, Warsaw, Berlin, Milan, London, Prague, Budapest, Johannesburg, Chicago and Cairo for a telephone conference in case of need. Petkov and Babourkov greeted the team members and Petkov took the floor.

Stanislav: 'Hello everybody. Peter and I are happy to be with you today. I am sorry to place so much stress on this meeting. It's probably because we've been working on 241E for over two years since the decision of the Board to approve the working concept of the new product. We have made all sorts of laboratory and market tests, and over 10 changes in the prototype since Cologne 2001. The team members and Peter Babourkov and I have had all sorts of discussions in this format. We even sold over 1,600 units of 241E while testing it in the markets. In our previous meetings we agreed upon almost everything, except on the end-user pricing. I refer to our marketing policy, which is based upon setting end-user prices, which are mandatory for all our sales companies and for the independent distributors. There are several options for setting our prices. As you will all agree, it is a matter of positioning our product in the markets. Once we position it, we can't change it very easily. The problem is to find the best price. It must give us a chance to sell a lot, without missing profits which we would have missed if our price was fixed below what the market would accept as a good price. We want your suggestions before we make the decision. Please speak your minds. In our work until now we have been driven to some extent by the positive reaction of our trading companies and other independent distributors. Peter and I are not afraid to make decisions related to the positioning of 241E on the basis of the initial, although very positive reactions, without considering all other circumstances.'

'Let us listen to Peter Atanassov first, then to Nikolay Ganchev in his capacity as Chief Designer of 241E, to Ivo Babushkin and Slava Dimova on the marketing point of view and the advertising support, then Alex Vladimirov on the technical readiness of the product. Then we'll probably make a conference call to Nigel Blackhead to learn his final point of view about our strategy in the UK. As some of you might have heard, we must consider the specific situation there. Then we'll discuss. Peter, you have the floor.'

Peter: 'Thank you. I'll only summarise the facts from the report, which you know. First, our companies in Russia, Ukraine, Poland, the Czech Republic, Hungary and South Africa have already placed their new orders for 2002, which is clear proof of the qualities and market potential of 241E. We have been informed that Germany, Italy, Iran, Iraq, Turkey, Egypt and Macedonia will order in a month or so. The information from Nigel Blackhead indicates a very positive development in the UK although we might be forced to go for a private label there. All these facts give support to 241E. Second, the analysis of the Consulting Group shows that the laboratory tests and the market tests done by our colleagues in the countries which I already mentioned are good. I'm sorry, I should have mentioned that we got over twenty technical and other remarks and suggestions on the prototype and over ten of them led to changes in the product. To be frank, most of the remarks corresponded to our own suggestions and we were happy to have these changes made early. Nikolay Kalbov will probably agree that the professors from the consulting group have made a good job of coordinating the work on these changes. To conclude, the country managers of the Group approved the product. We have supplied all our local companies and partners distributors with catalogues and leaflets, as well as the required technical documentation. The advertising campaign is already on. Now we want to make a proposal on the price level. We think that if we want to sustain our image of a "professional quality at reasonable prices" company, we must fix for 241E a price level which is about 10% below the end-user prices of Bosch.'

Peter looked at the CEOs and continued:

'Let me take Russia as an example. Bosch is selling its rotary hammer with similar characteristics at 199 euro. If we agree upon a 10% lower price for our 241E this means a price level at about 179 euro, which seems to be a good price according to all our surveys and calculations. It will keep our image of a high ranking company offering very good quality at reasonable prices. But I want to use this opportunity to propose a radical decision for the price. After the analysis of the pricing policies of our main competitors in Russia and the other CIS countries our team – I mean, Nikolay Kalbov, the marketing people and I – believe that if we fix a price in the range of 169–179 euro we will make at least 20% more sales than if we fix it exactly at 179 euro. Our joint proposal for the CIS markets is the range between 169 and 179 euro, leaving each market the freedom to decide the particular end-user price after consultations with the country managers of SPARKY. This will clearly position us as one of the market leaders in terms of brand image and quality. About the other markets: well, we think that we must follow our regular policy of −10% compared to Bosch. All this is elaborated on in the files that you got this morning. Concerning the UK, we agree that our best bet is a private label strategy. Wickes is a very well known brand name in that market and we will sell much more under that name, compared with what we can achieve under the SPARKY brand name. We must take into consideration the negative connotation of the word "sparky" for British consumers.'

Stanislav: 'OK. Nikolay Ganchev, brief us about the latest changes in the product please.'

Nikolay: 'We haven't made any changes of the prototype since the last Board meeting. There was no need to make any. As already reported to you, we have taken into consideration all remarks and suggestions and all reasonable and feasible changes have been made. We believe that this product now is far superior to the prototype in 2001. It is also considerably more reliable.'

Stanislav: 'Good. Ivo and Slava, would you like to add something to this from the marketing point of view?'

Ivo Babushkin (Marketing Manager): 'Well, we participated in all stages of the process. This time the designers agreed with almost all suggestions after the laboratory and the market tests. We also think that the consumers will find 241E to be a very good product, which satisfies their needs and preferences even better than most of the competitors. The advertising campaign can support and even push up the sales with such a pricing policy. It corresponds fully to our general positioning policy and we support it.'

'Kalbov, do you support this information and the proposal for the prices?'

Nikolay: 'Yes. I even signed the paper along with the other members of the team. I would like in particular to bring your attention to the proposal for a price range between 169 and 179 euro. It will give us additional advantage over the competitors compared to other pricing levels. It is important for us. After all, there are not so many well paid professionals in Russia.'

'Would you elaborate a bit on the sales forecast? Russia first, as it would account for about half of the sales forecasts, but also the other markets?' Peter Babourkov, the other CEO of SPARKY Group, asked.

Stanislav: 'How much will the profit be if we go for 175 euro? I am taking it as an average between 169 and 179.'

'Based on what Yuri Listratov reports as a forecast for Russia, we believe that we'll be able to reach sales of 100,000 hammers in 2002. With the marketing support which we have already we expect some 25% increase in sales each year until we reach about 200,000 hammers a year. Then we expect saturation for 1–2 years followed by decline. The product lifecycle will not be longer than 5–6 years. By that time we believe we will have launched a new model. Concerning the profit: we expect about 10% at those end-user prices for Russia, CIS and the middle European markets.'

Stanislav: 'OK. What about Western Europe? We do not sell only to Russia and the CIS.'

Atanassov: 'Yes, of course. Tilo Germer from Germany and Vassil Kovandjiysky from South Africa worked with us on the document. We all agree that in

West Europe and in South Africa we have a pure brand competition and the price must correspond to the consumer's perception about the brand name. From what we understand from you, Mr Petkov and Mr Babourkov, in the UK we must go for a private label with Wickes. According to Tilo Germer you, I mean you as CEOs of the Group, have prepared an agreement for Germany since the negotiations last week. Probably not everybody knows the problem, namely that Otto Versant and OBI are merging and the current agreement needs an approval from the new Board. So except for the UK and Germany we propose: −10% of the prices of Bosch in each particular market for all such markets listed in the document. For the UK and Germany we must listen to our CEOs first.'

Stanislav: 'OK. Let us brief you on the situation in Germany and we'll call Nigel in London for his hot information on the UK. As you know Mr Babourkov and I had talks with the new vice president of the new Otto and OBI. Finally we agreed to reinforce our current contract. Peter and I believe that this is our best possible strategy for Germany. The prices could have been better, but we decided to accept them, thus sacrificing the profit per unit sold for the amount of sales. We propose to stick to our general pricing strategy for all other sales in Germany.'

Stanislav: 'Peter, would you get Nigel on the phone please? Let's see what Wickes have to say.'

Peter Babourkov was already calling the UK SPARKY country manager:

Peter: 'Hello, Nigel. Can you talk? Good. We are discussing our positioning strategy for 241E, as you know. Did you get the answer from Wickes?'

Babourkov pressed the button for conference talk so that everybody could listen to the words of Nigel Blackhead.

Nigel: 'Hello, everybody! As a matter of fact I got the answer about a half hour ago but I did not call you so as not to interrupt the Board meeting. The answer is positive. They invited our CEOs to sign the contract within the next two weeks so that the first regular delivery could be made by the end of April. I have always supported the idea that the private label is our best strategy for the UK. Do not think that I'm looking for the easiest strategy. It's just that in the UK things are different from the rest of Europe. So, congratulations.'

Peter (looking at people in the room): 'Thank you Nigel. Are there any questions to Nigel?'

'No? Nigel, thank you again; Stanislav and I will call you tomorrow to fix the details about our visit to London next week.'

Then Babourkov switched off the phone.

Stanislav: 'Good. The UK is clear. Germany as well, I believe. Let's get back to all other markets, where we sell over 90% of what we produce. Can we back up all these radiant forecasts for sales with production? Alex and Nikolay, do you confirm that the production facilities can handle the supply schedule of 241E along with the production schedule for the other products?'

Nikolay: 'Yes, we do.' Alex Vladimirov also nodded to confirm.

Stanislav: 'OK. On the basis of what everybody here said and on the basis of the results of the surveys presented in the materials in our files this Board approves the proposal for positioning of 241E as a product of professional quality and at a price −10% off the end-user prices of Bosch in all markets except Russia and the CIS countries. There we'll apply a price between 169 and 179 euro. Peter Atanassov and Yuri Listratov will have the right to decide on the actual prices depending upon the buyer. In the UK we go for a private label with Wickes. In Germany we go for a distribution contract with Otto and OBI. Thank you gentlemen. You've done a great work on the development of the product and on its launch. Push all pedals to make these plans happen.'

This case is used with the permission of the CEO of the SPARKY Group and I gratefully acknowledge their generosity in allowing the material to be cited. All names used in this case, except one, are real.

Summary and conclusion

Despite its COMECON background, marketing has been developed and applied in Bulgaria for over 30 years. Evidently, marketing was initially associated with exporting, but after the political upheavals of the early 1990s, and especially after the privatisation of over 80 per cent of all companies, it has now become almost a household word.

However, in many cases, companies and institutions do not apply the marketing concept in the manner perhaps anticipated in advanced Western nations. This is partly due to lack of market and statistical information and partly due to lack of finance for marketing intelligence. In many cases, there are executives and managers who misinterpret and misuse marketing methods and instruments, which leads to enhanced market risk by companies, while simultaneously damaging fragile consumer loyalties.

The two cases illustrate the application of the marketing concept using the rhetoric and reality construct. The first case, concerning the Pink Wafer, depicts a scenario of marketing mimicry, which does resemble to a degree what the application of marketing might suggest. It does represent a real case, though with a disguised brand name. Here, while the marketing concept is mentioned, the application of marketing relies on carrying out market analysis in a very off-hand

and slip-shod manner. The decision to proceed with new product and packaging development is not based on any real understanding of the dynamics of the market served. And yet, based on the materials in this chapter, many old-style marketing approaches may have continued into the new-style companies of the 1990s and beyond. What is being applied is a form of rhetoric, while many realities of marketing are being ignored. The Pink Wafer product seems almost doomed to failure. Plainly, the company and its staff have a long way to go in terms of turning marketing from rhetoric into reality.

The second case, SPARKY's electric hand-tools, presents the marketing decision-making process in a company which has been very successful in applying the marketing concept in one of their major businesses. As a result of active marketing and innovation SPARKY Group has been able to develop its image and gain market share in 40–50 countries, to which it exports electric hand-tools. This case draws close to the accepted dynamics of *marketing* reality, whereas the first case is more illustrative of an organisation adopting marketing almost as a form of window dressing. Here, customer and consumer needs play a dynamic role in product formulation and design. Competitive and other environmental forces are carefully analysed in each market. A lengthy new product development process is followed by extensive meetings, and the decision to launch is carefully buttressed and underpinned by market intelligence. Each component of the marketing mix is planned in a manner resembling a carefully orchestrated military campaign. Here we have an example of a company exposed to all the usual market forces, rapidly grasping the realities of the marketing concept, and applying the necessary strategic and tactical decisions to make it work for them. It is an excellent example of what is described elsewhere in this book as 'the reality of marketing'.

These cases present two different faces of marketing practice. Both are useful for analysis and drawing conclusions about implementing the marketing discipline. Readers may choose whether they prefer the rhetoric or reality of marketing.

Appendix

Table A8.1 Output of some industrial products 1990–93 (1990 = 100%)				
Industrial products	1990 (%)	1991 (%)	1992 (%)	1993 (%)
Metallurgy				
1 Iron ores (100% content Fe)	100	56.7	74.5	82.7
2 Manganese ores (100% content Mn)	100	79.1	62.7	36.4
3 Steel	100	73.9	71.0	88.9
4 Rolled stock	100	60.7	61.0	72.1
5 Steel pipes	100	41.8	38.0	39.4
6 Coke	100	53.6	61.0	66.3
7 Electrolyte copper	100	52.7	74.1	108.2
8 Lead	100	84.4	79.7	85.6
9 Zinc	100	77.7	76.6	71.4
10 Tin	100	34.4	35.9	34.4
11 Aluminium	100	45.1	59.0	26.6
Machine tools				
12 Internal combustion engines	100	22.6	22.2	11.8
13 Lathes	100	94.6	71.5	43.6
14 Drilling machines	100	41.4	21.1	16.1
15 Shaping machines	100	72.4	112.5	82.8
16 Electric hoists	100	21.5	5.4	5.6
17 Electric fork lift trucks	100	57.1	17.8	11.1
18 Motor fork lift trucks	100	35.4	25.6	10.2
Electrical machines				
19 Electric motors	100	54.5	39.3	32.3
20 Electric generators	100	138.0	73.5	53.0
21 Power transformers	100	95.5	55.9	20.1
22 Storage batteries	100	56.2	55.3	49.1
23 Telephones	100	56.8	15.3	14.8
24 Radio sets	100	37.4	11.1	1.9
25 Television sets (colour)	100	28.9	18.2	6.1
26 Washing machines (household)	100	81.7	76.2	46.2
27 Refrigerators	100	79.7	129.9	99.6
28 Electric ovens	100	36.4	76.7	45.5
29 Insulated copper wires	100	57.2	62.2	59.3
30 Cables	100	45.5	57.3	65.1
Chemicals				
31 Synthetic ammonia (100% N)	100	83.5	69.1	67.6
32 Nitrogen fertilisers (100% N)	100	83.5	71.7	67.1
33 Phosphate fertilisers (100% P_2O_2)	100	79.2	80.0	96.6
34 Soda ash (98% NaOH)	100	85.4	49.4	24.8
35 Sulphuric acid (mono hydrate)	100	68.2	77.5	78.3
36 Caustic soda (96% HaOH)	100	70.7	65.9	44.9
37 Pesticides (100% active ingredients)	100	97.0	72.0	83.0
38 Diesel oil	100	51.9	24.0	30.0
39 Plastic, synthetic resins and adhesives	100	58.4	56.7	64.7
40 Chemical fibres	100	44.2	60.6	53.4

Cont'd

Table A8.1 cont'd

Industrial products	1990 (%)	1991 (%)	1992 (%)	1993 (%)
Building materials				
41 Cement	100	51.1	44.7	42.6
42 Prefabricated ferroconcrete	100	13.4	10.3	7.2
Wood processing				
43 Bricks	100	67.4	66.0	61.0
44 Round and split timber	100	65.9	68.6	74.6
45 Coniferous boards	100	47.7	32.2	20.6
46 Non-coniferous boards	100	65.6	61.0	43.5
47 Plywood	100	52.2	44.6	47.2
48 veneer	100	57.1	39.4	25.3
Cellulose and paper				
49 Cellulose	100	75.8	71.8	55.3
50 Paper	100	58.9	46.6	45.8
Glass				
51 Plate glass (base 2 mm)	100	83.8	64.9	51.3
Textile and knitwear				
52 Cotton yarn	100	42.9	35.3	27.6
53 Woollen yarn	100	61.7	53.0	47.7
54 Hemp and flax yarn	100	53.4	21.9	6.8
55 Cotton fabrics	100	43.4	30.8	24.2
56 Woollen fabrics	100	55.1	48.1	48.7
57 Silk fabrics	100	49.6	41.9	40.5
58 Hemp and flax fabrics	100	41.0	43.8	17.1
59 Knitwear	100	51.5	38.2	23.2
60 Knitted underwear	100	40.1	31.4	22.1
61 Clothing	100	57.7	29.0	14.3
Leather and footwear				
62 Soft leather	100	63.2	55.6	42.2
63 Fur	100	70.4	44.4	29.6
64 Leather footwear	100	57.4	49.3	39.0
Food, beverages and tobacco				
65 Meat	100	56.9	43.5	19.9
66 Canned vegetables	100	75.7	33.3	32.3
67 Canned fruit	100	38.1	23.5	18.2
68 Butter	100	57.4	40.3	19.9
69 White cheese	100	85.0	60.9	40.7
70 Yellow cheese	100	73.8	55.8	41.0
71 Vegetable oils	100	77.3	94.5	106.2
72 Flour	100	88.3	73.5	67.7
73 Rice	100	48.9	36.4	40.2
74 Sugar	100	68.1	52.8	54.4
75 Sugar products	100	65.7	70.1	69.7
76 Brandy	100	131.7	164.3	88.4
77 Wine	100	111.0	91.3	49.7
78 Beer	100	75.0	72.1	64.9
79 Tobacco products	100	105.1	64.1	42.3

Chapter 9

The rhetoric and reality of marketing in India

ashish sadh and sharada tangirala

Introduction

A snapshot of India:

- one billion population
- ranks seventh in the world in area
- ranks first in the world in irrigated area
- ranks second in production of rice, wheat, milk and sugar
- ranks twelfth for GDP
- ranks eighth in electricity generation
- ranks thirtieth in exports of goods and services

(*Source: TATA Statistical Outline of India 2000–2001*)

This chapter attempts to unravel and explain the following key issues in the Indian context:

- an insight into the Indian consumer
- recent practices in marketing products and services in India
- adherence to the marketing concept and managerial commitment to satisfy the needs and wants of target customers by four case examples that illustrate clear organisational allegiance to the marketing concept

- further examples of companies who, though marketing-oriented in other nations, have nonetheless adopted marketing as a form of rhetoric in India

- illustrative trends of the rhetoric/reality construct in the context of the 4 Ps of marketing

The process used to put together this chapter has been an explorative investigation of the issues using several instances and cases, in order to develop actual facts and situations. The rationale for using multiple cases, rather than two as is the case with other chapters, is to provide readers with illustrative examples of the diversity and range of marketing activities and its possibilities in this, the second most populated country on earth.

An insight into the Indian consumer

The Indian market consists of about a billion people, where every 200–300 kilometres provides a different language or dialect, different cuisine, different cultural perspectives, and different styles of classical music, dance and folklore. There are also significant differences in buyer behaviour to satisfy similar human needs. Around 40 per cent of the population speak the national language, Hindi, with the balance speaking over 15 other key languages (see Table 9.1). English is spoken mainly in urban areas and a significant 10–12 per cent of the urban population read English language newspapers or magazines. But underneath the diversity is a shared patriotic spirit, by and large a secular religious sentiment, a reverence for Indian mythological and religious epics (*Mahabharata, Ramayana, Bhaghavadgītā*), a common passion for cricket and for three-hour long local movies filled with song and dance! Icons in India are film stars, cricketers and MTV veejays (MTV India incidentally is now completely Indianised).

This is a country where well over 70 per cent of the population still lives in rural areas (the 2001 census gave a total population of 1,027,015,247, of which 741,660,293 were rural) but it is also a country where 72,000 luxury cars, each costing over Rs12 lakhs, were bought in 2001 (12 lakhs = approximately US$24,000+). It is surprising to know that a 30,000 strong crowd turned up to rock to the music of Roger Walters (of Pink Floyd fame) in Bangalore City in South India (see Figures 9.1 and 9.2, which compare and contrast a slice of urban and rural life).

Table 9.1	Languages spoken in India
Language	**Percentage**
Hindi	40.22
Bengali	8.30
Telugu	7.87
Marathi	7.45
Tamil	6.32
Urdu	5.18
Gujarati	4.85
Kannada	3.91
Malayalam	3.62
Oriya	3.35
Punjabi	2.79
Assamese	1.56
Sindhi	0.25
Nepali	0.25
Konkani	0.21
Manipuri	0.15
Kashmiri	0.01
Sanskrit	0.01
Other languages	3.71
Total	100.00

Source: 1991 census of India (base population 838, 583, 988).

Figure 9.1   Mumbai's famous Marine Drive facing the Arabian Sea with high rise buildings and rush hour traffic

Figure 9.2 Rural folk gathered against the backdrop of typical village dwellings/huts

For marketers, it is a well-known fact that coverage of retail units to make a significant dent in this market runs into several hundred thousand outlets, the total number of outlets being 5.5 million. Most companies even today target mainly the urban market due to distribution problems in reaching the large but location-wise isolated rural areas (see Appendix 9.1).

Urban India is characterised by a pyramid-shaped income structure (see Figure 9.3) with a large poor-base, a significant middle class running into 150 million (who are the consuming class for most packaged goods and durables/services), and a small top end of well-heeled, high-income households who are quite different from the middle class in terms of aspirations and lifestyle. To illustrate further these gaps, the large lower end of the socio-economic structure buys whatever they can afford and they have a lot of unfulfilled aspirations; the consuming middle class are price-sensitive and quality-conscious; while the top end have 'affordability' and go about acquiring whatever happens to be the latest status symbol (Sangameshwaran, 2002).

This introduction, in a nutshell, describes India's partly homogeneous, partly heterogeneous masses which are spread over 28 states and seven union territories (see Figure 9.4, the map of India).

India is most often described as an emerging market with the potential to become an economic superpower in a couple of decades.

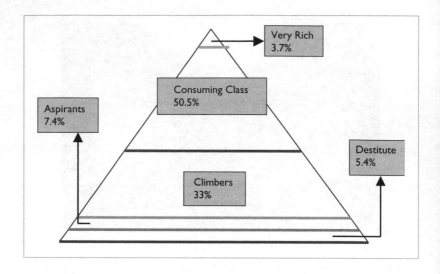

Figure 9.3   Indian urban market structure
Population breakdown by National Council of Applied Economic Research
(NCAER) for 2000–1.

Liberalisation took shape in the early 1990s and brought back Coca-Cola which had left India in the 1970s. From the 1990s onwards, the floodgates have opened wide and many multinational corporations (such as Levi, Wrigley's and Kellogg's, to name a few) have entered the market.

Recent practices in marketing products and services in India

Let us look at several cases and examples drawn from Indian public sector/private sector and multinational firms and, through the trials, tribulations and triumphs of these companies, try to compose a coherent picture of marketing practices in the subcontinent. We have attempted to draw lessons from the strategies of some of these businesses and to highlight the significant impact, if any, that these companies are making on the marketing paradigm in India. While one may find that there is no one archetypal formula to serve all sectors of this market, there does emerge a pattern of prerequisites successfully to enter, survive and grow in the Indian market. We will consider some of the marketing successes and some marketing mishaps in the course of understanding the marketing concept in the Indian context.

Figure 9.4   Map of India

The year 2001 saw the creation of three new states in India taking the total number of states from 25 to 28.

Source: Office of the Registrar General India, 2A, Mansingh Road, New Delhi 110 011, India; *rgoffice@censusindia.net,* created 9 November 2001.

A close look at detailed case examples of marketing reality

These companies will comprise:

- Hindustan Lever Limited (HLL): the Indian arm of the Anglo-Dutch FMCG multinational Unilever

- TATA Group: a home-grown Indian company started in the 19th century

■ Amul: a cooperative sector brand that charted an unprecedented course for itself in the development of milk products

■ Jet Airways: a rapidly growing player in the air-passenger market, which seems to have done its homework where marketing is concerned

Apart from these four companies the chapter will later present other vignettes including Kellogg's (a multinational breakfast cereal manufacturer); BPL (a consumer durable company); and Nirma (a local player who gave HLL a run for its money in the detergent market), besides others.

Hindustan Lever Limited (HLL)

This company registered profit after tax of Rs1641 crores for the year 2001 (a profit growth of 25.3 per cent) and its net sales for the year were Rs.10,972 crores (US$2.29 billion) registering a growth of 3.5 per cent, making it the largest FMCG player in India. Profitable growth was driven by HLL's new strategy of focusing on power brands. Unilever has recently introduced the concept of focusing on their identified 'power brands'. In India HLL plans to focus on 30 power brands, which are major contributors to profitability: 'One of our major strategic thrusts is to grow the business by focusing resources behind 30 power brands. We have redefined the market in all the categories we operate in. We have also redirected our innovation activity towards leading market development' stated M.S. Banga, chairman of Hindustan Lever in 2001. This section traces the building of a few key brands in their portfolio in India.

The marketing concept at work in HLL
HLL is the most admired Indian marketing company in the FMCG category. It is said that marketing at HLL is obsessive and runs from product idea generation to buying an advertising spot. HLL constantly tracks a large number of consumers every year. Consumer research is one of the major sources for new product ideas. What follows are some of the research activities usually undertaken at HLL:

■ Post-launch studies

■ Sales tracking

■ Trial and repurchase trends

- Advertising recall and attitudes
- Brand image associations

A close look at HLL over the years shows that the company has used a combination of proactive *and* reactive measures in its marketing history in India. By this one means that the company has been proactive in anticipating and understanding consumer needs and wants in many instances, and has been reactive in some instances after a competitor has identified a particular need and been successful in meeting it.

Proactive examples
These include *product innovation,* such as the 'Fair & Lovely' brand which is a unique concept in personal care in the subcontinent and surrounding countries (this brand is discussed in detail later in the chapter); and also ready to eat chapattis (Indian bread) which are an acknowledgement that modern Indian women are increasingly seeking convenience.

Another example is *rural programmes*: already, half of HLL's sales in soaps and detergents come from rural markets. There is still enormous potential to build an even larger market through higher penetration. HLL's commitment to understanding rural consumers goes back a long way, with every Lever management trainee spending six to eight weeks in a rural village, eating, sleeping, and talking with the locals. Marketing executives also make frequent two-day visits to low-income areas. To quote M.S. Banga again, whose tenure with the company began in such a village: 'Once you spend time with consumers, you realise that they want the same things you want. They want a good quality of life.'

Third, there is *commitment to R&D*: research ranges from refining high-end shampoos to developing mass-market products such as low-cost ice-creams and low-cost soaps.

Fourth, there are *new services*: for instance, Lakme Beauty Salons. From being simply a manufacturer, this chain has begun to introduce services leveraging the equity of its brands, such as Lakme.

Fifth, we have the opportunity to *explore new media choices*, such as touch-screen kiosks in supermarkets for information on the Lakme range of cosmetics and beauty products, and the use of the Internet as a support medium in a consumer promotion for ice-creams.

Sixth, there are *major acquisitions*. Forays into the ice-cream market were made in the 1990s with the acquisition of the largest player in the Indian ice-cream market, Kwality, and the launch of Kwality Walls with several other international brands in the Walls range. Instead of setting up a complex, capital-intensive cold chain distribution system, HLL chose to pick up the 'readymade' facilities of Kwality, besides acquiring the highly recognised 'Kwality' brand name. A subsequent first in the Indian market was the low-cost vitaminised ice-creams for children in the MAX range.

Then there are *brands at different price points*, which are a range of brands catering to different income segments at different price points in soaps, teas, and so on.

Eighth, there is the possibility of *developing a niche with direct sales under the Aviance brand*. The use of direct selling in exclusive FMCG products is characterized by low distribution costs and advertising expenditure spend since most communications and sales are done through direct selling agents on a commission basis. These agents, who are usually middle-class homemakers, identify and cultivate potential customers.

Ninth, there is the chance to *explore branding opportunities in commodities*. HLL redefined competition to include unorganised sectors in wheat, flour and salt products. HLL entered several of these product categories which were perceived as commodities and difficult to differentiate on the basis of product attributes, and became successful in them.

Finally, *building enduring brands*: HLL has been the highest advertising spender in the mass media for several years now and strives to sustain and build brands through a constant process of re-launch and innovation. These re-launches are either based on product improvement or refreshing the communication platform, and are labelled 'minor/major innovation' in the company lexicon worldwide (including India). Based on multinational experience elsewhere, HLL executives were quick to recognise the power of television in the 1980s when the growth of the medium started in India. Today, a majority of their advertising spend is via television, which is a mass (and still high-involvement) medium among homemakers, who are a core target group for most HLL brands.

Reactive measures
The launching of a low-priced detergent called 'Wheel' by HLL to tackle the local entrant, known as 'Nirma', came many months

after Nirma hit the market. Nirma Limited, an Indian company incorporated in 1980, gave HLL a run for its money in detergents. The Nirma brand is associated with low-cost 'value for money' and is popular in the lower-medium segment of the market. Nirma is today the second-largest manufacturer of detergents in volume *and* value terms but second to HLL in value terms. Nirma started as a detergent manufacturer before expanding into soaps, toothpaste, salt and raw material inputs. The brand has an estimated 35 per cent volume share of the synthetic detergents, cakes and bars market in India.

The launch of shampoo in sachets came after a regional player had pioneered the concept. Chik Shampoo started marketing shampoo in sachets in the early 1990s. This became an instant hit with consumers due to the low unit cost and the convenience of use for a single wash. Shampoo sachets typically come in 8–10 ml plastic units; a consumer simply has to cut and pour, and the sachets are affordably priced at a couple of Indian rupees. HLL subsequently entered the sachet segment for all its shampoo brands. Besides tapping the lower end of the urban market, low unit packs also penetrate rural areas. Now, sachets account for about 70 per cent of shampoo market sales in India, and one-third of India's shampoo sales in 2000 came from sachet sales in rural India. HLL now has 70 per cent of those rural sales. A counter-competitive measure was Clinic Active, a shampoo variant introduced with an additional 'Pro V' ingredient (vitamin B5) to counter competitor P&G's Pantene Pro V5.

All in all, HLL is considered a formidable player in the Indian market with a huge consumer base through several well-recognised brands. This is a clear example of a division of a multinational company that has adopted a consumer-focused approach, that has integrated marketing at all levels of business activity, and whose brands have gained widespread acceptance on the Indian subcontinent. Note, however, that marketing reality invariably involves not just a focus on consumers and satisfying their needs, but also the ability to respond to competitive threats as well. A few examples of HLL's focus on customer and their needs are described below.

Fair & Lovely

Fair & Lovely is a personal care brand based on a patented breakthrough in skin lightening technology and has been marketed in India since the late 1970s (see Figure 9.5). The brand caters to the unique

Figure 9.5   'Fair & Lovely', a brand from HLL

social need among Asian women for fair skin. The formulation has been researched and constantly improved upon over the years. Fair & Lovely currently contains a unique fairness system that is a combination of active agents and sunscreens. This has been specially designed to deliver one to three shades of change in most people. Also its sunscreen system is created specially for Indian skin which, unlike Caucasian skin, tends to 'tan' rather than 'burn', requiring a different combination of UV A and UV B sunscreens.

This fairness cream has now been marketed in over 38 countries through HLL Exports and local Unilever companies, and has become the largest-selling skin lightening cream in the world. The brand has extensions such as Fair & Lovely Fairness Reviving Lotion, Fair & Lovely Fairness Cold Cream, Fair & Lovely Under-Eye Cream, and Fair & Lovely Fairness Soap. The success of the brand led to several 'me-too's in the market, but Fair and Lovely continues to be the market leader.

Close-Up
This is a toothpaste gel brand that fosters the individuality of youth, so the young do not have to use the same brand as their parents. Through most of the 1990s the brand was built on the fresh breath position targeted at the young with ads which asked consumers to do the 'hah hah' test (i.e., blowing on to the palm as a fresh breath test). The communication style for this brand is trendy, upbeat, full of fun and laughter and usually portrays a teenage boy and girl situation with the apt tag line 'Close-Up is for close ups'! (See Appendix 9.2, Generation Next.)

Clinic Plus: product upgrading and brand extensions
Clinic Plus shampoo was launched in 1972, and is positioned for the entire family. The brand has been upgraded several times over the years. The shampoo is targeted towards families. Most middle-class households in India have the tendency to pick up one affordable shampoo that can provide healthy hair for the entire family. It is still Clinic Plus which hold the key to the Clinic brand's success in India.

Next came the re-launch of an earlier brand extension, Clinic Special, as Clinic All Clear. Traditionally dandruff shampoos in India have been perceived as expensive and harsh on the hair. Clinic All Clear was given a cosmetic feel.

P&G brought in Head & Shoulders in mid-1997, with 'ZPT', an anti-microbial agent. Three months later, it extended Pantene to anti-dandruff uses. HLL countered this move by introducing a similar technology with Clinic All Clear backed by a two-week challenge that the brand can get rid of dandruff within two weeks. Using youth icon and film idol Shah Rukh Khan in the Clinic All Clear campaign was reported to have boosted sales and market share.

Brand extension into hair oil was the next step. While Clinic Plus offered a non-sticky coconut oil, the All Clear franchise was extended to a perfumed dandruff hair oil. In 2001 Clinic Plus was relaunched with an added supplement of 'protein health complex'. In 2002, HLL once again refreshed the brand with a 'protein serum'.

The Clinic story is one where HLL strives to offer variants to cater to different segments of the market, has upgraded the offering with improved ingredients and extended its brand's franchise to other hair care products.

Lifebuoy: a mass market brand
Way back in 1884, a new washing substance was born, when an acid added to the residue of Sunlight laundry soap made by Lever Bros led to a new formulation that took the name Lifebuoy and entered the Indian market as a bath soap around 1895. For this brand, HLL started out by targeting rural consumers, many of whom (at that time) did not use branded soap but rather traditional cleaning material or local unbranded soap. HLL drew attention to personal hygiene issues and priced Lifebuoy lower than most soaps. The brand, with a carbolic content, was eventually successful in garnering a mass market in the rural areas. The first Lifebuoy bar was a red, box-shaped 150 g cake,

with a disinfectant-like smell. It was packaged in a plain red-and-white wrapper, and came with a promise of eliminating all germs.

By 1992, the sales of Lifebuoy exceeded 125,000 tonnes, a figure unmatched by any other soap in the market.

As an economy brand the rural success was largely among a male target group. In fact the users in urban areas were also lower-income working-class men and the brand did not find favour among housewives and young adults because its image did not complement these segments.

A handwash variant called Liquid Lifebuoy was launched in 1993, to target the upper-income urbanites. Packaged in a 250 ml pump dispenser, it was a first of sorts. Many variants and extensions of the original product (such as Lifebuoy Plus and Lifebuoy Gold) have been launched to cater to the popular and premium segment soap users in urban areas. Lifebuoy Gold soap was in complete contrast to Lifebuoy's earlier image, though the promise was the same: it eliminated all germs. Perfumed and white in colour, the new soap was appreciated. Despite competition from Reckitt & Benkiser's Dettol soap and J&J's Savlon soap on the hygiene-through-germ-fighting platform, Lifebuoy is still way ahead of the competition. The most recent change in Lifebuoy is a move away from its carbolic soap position (which consumers no longer identify with) to a milled toilet soap with a simple 'fights germs' position.

Lifebuoy has been among the top brands in India (especially in the rural segment) for a long time. Lifebuoy has changed with the times and it reflects HLL's commitment to be as contemporary as possible in catering to consumer needs and wants.

TATA

The company's web site proudly proclaims 'Leadership with trust' alongside the well-recognised TATA logo. India's largest business house has 80 companies, 230,000 employees, 2 million shareholders and a turnover of Rs.41,300 crores (US$8.8 billion). The TATA Group interests span a diverse mix including tele-services, salt, automobiles, steel, watches and software development. We will look at TATA's company philosophy, mission and goals in general and the marketing concept in practice for one of their high-profile brands, Titan, a watch brand which rewrote the rules of marketing watches in India.

The TATA Group has many firsts to its credit giving it a leadership position in many industries. It is now:

- Asia's largest software exporter
- India's largest private sector steel producer
- the owner of the largest five-star chain of luxury hotels in India
- India's largest manufacturer of soda ash
- India's largest private sector power utility

The TATA Group has done much in terms of trailblazing business development. They:

- pioneered India's steel industry
- started the first power plant in India
- pioneered civil aviation in India
- brought insurance to India
- started India's first chain of luxury hotels
- led India's software development efforts
- launched India's first quartz watches
- introduced labour welfare benefits long before they were enacted by law (provident fund, gratuity, maternity benefits)

Their web site proclaims a marketing purpose and allegiance:

> At the TATA Group our purpose is to improve the quality of life of the communities we serve. We do this through leadership in sectors of national economic significance, to which the group brings a unique set of capabilities. This requires us to grow aggressively in focused areas of business. Our heritage of returning to society what we earn evokes trust among consumers, employees, shareholders and the community. This heritage will be continuously enriched by formalizing the high standards of behavior expected from employees and companies. The TATA name is a unique asset representing 'leadership with trust'. Leveraging this asset to enhance group synergy and becoming globally competitive is the route to sustained growth and long-term success.

Titan Industries

Titan Industries Limited is a joint venture of the TATA Group and The Tamil Nadu Industrial Development Corporation (TIDCO).

Part of the TATA Group, the Titan brand of watches completely rewrote the rules of the game. The company is rated as the most admired marketing company of India in the consumer durable category. Titan entered a market monopolised by a well-entrenched public sector company, Hindustan Machine Tools (HMT), positioned as 'the time keepers to the nation'. Titan Industries, which entered in the 1980s, now enjoys close to a 50 per cent share among nationally recognised brands. While HMT continues to be a significant player, its market is now largely rural and semi-urban. Titan Industries watches are presently sold in about 40 countries through marketing subsidiaries based in London, Dubai and Singapore. They enjoy a reputation for being excellent value for money. Titan Industries also makes watches for international labels.

Tracing the development of Titan
Below is some information about the Titan brand:

- it is a range of watches to suit every pocket and spanning from low price to higher-end stylish premium watches
- the range of designs is far superior to HMT's offering in aesthetical appeal, contemporary design, and trendiness
- it is noted for workmanship and reliability

Besides the superiority of the product in appearance and style, marketing communication played a big role in rejuvenating the category and instantly repositioned watches from being functional timepieces to fashion accessories. The company used the gifting route in well produced television commercials to create an emotional bond between the brand and consumers. The images, the music, the superior quality production values and the extensive use of the growing television medium ensured that Titan not only became a household name, but a name any Indian was proud to be associated with. The Titan brand metamorphosed the entire industry. What was a 'once-in-a-lifetime' purchase is today a multiple ownership category. It is now fairly common for Indians to own two or more watches to suit different situations in their lifestyle. From the year 2000, Titan intends to make inroads into the vast rural market with 'Sonata', its brand for the mass market. Titan sees rural India 'as a market waiting for the marketer'.

To quote Mr Xerxes Desai, the ex-Vice Chairman of the company (quoted while in office during 2000): 'There is a dangerous, urban, elitist approach to categorize rural India as some solid mass when there is actually a need properly to segment and classify this market.' He believes that the rural market is even more diverse than the urban one with highly differing lifestyles between the rich and poor.

The company has been selling to its rural customers through urban distribution (i.e., rural customers who visit larger towns have access to Titan's products). Titan has conducted research into the rural market in order to develop its marketing and to have a focused entry with a specific product, specific communication and distribution for this market.

Titan executives believe that the rural market needs a completely different communication exercise to be effective. In addition to hiring research agencies such as MODE, Titan has worked with companies that have done extensive work in rural markets (such as TI Cycles) to get a better understanding of rural consumers.

The main competitor for Titan in the rural watch markets is from its traditional rival, HMT, which already has a franchise in this market and whose brand is popularly known as 'Chemti' watches, an Indianised pronunciation of HMT.

Achievements
Titan Industries Limited is recognised as a corporate leader by its professional peers. It has been ranked as India's leading consumer durables marketing company for the past seven years in polls conducted by the country's leading advertising and marketing publication, *A&M*. It was rated as one of Asia's top 200 companies and was in India's top 10 in each of the years 1994 to 1998 in surveys conducted by *The Far Eastern Economic Review*. In another survey conducted by *The Economic Times* in the year 2000, Titan was voted India's most admired brand. Recognition has come in several forms for the company's engineering capabilities, innovative products, advertising excellence and services to the community

Amul

Amul Butter was launched in 1945. It is today a well recognised brand in milk, butter and other milk products. Amul was the trade name of Kaira District Milk Co-operative Producers' Union who pioneered the co-operative dairy industry in India. Gujarat Co-operative Milk Marketing Federation (GCMMF) was the marketing arm of this set-up. GCMMF launched the Amul brand, but it was only in the mid-1960s that the brand started gaining prominence, after the introduction of the 'utterly butterly delicious' tag line with the Amul girl as a graphic identifier and catchy lines in their communication. This strategy worked especially well on their billboards where the 'tongue-in-cheek' catchy lines changed frequently with topical news or events such as cricket scores, political happenings or even Hindi films. A play of words on Sachin Tendulkar winning a car for the cricket finals between India and Australia is shown in Figure 9.6.

There has been no looking back since then. Amul has had a virtual monopoly in India's butter market for years. Amul started focusing on milk products in the 1980s. In the mid-1990s, the management adopted total quality management (TQM) and set for itself higher benchmarks in terms of growth. The strategy included diversification of Amul to milk-based foodstuffs such as ice-cream, condensed milk, cheese, Indian sweets and much more. Amul launched its own range of ice-creams in 1997 after Hindustan Lever's acquisition of Kwality. Amul ice-cream is positioned as the 'Real Ice-cream' as against Kwality Walls' position as a frozen dessert. For the last five years, the challenge has been to expand the consumption base of milk-based products in India. The range of brands launched has been

Figure 9.6   One of the Amul billboards

communicated through a single Amul brand commercial (a multi-product range advertisement instead of separate ads for each product) with the very apt base line 'Amul, The Taste of India'. One advantage Amul enjoys over its rivals is in pricing. Amul's products are priced 20–40 per cent lower than other brands, thereby firmly establishing presence among the mass middle-income, price-sensitive consumers. Quality, right pricing and 'a taste of India' is what Amul is all about (Koshy and Sinha, 1999).

Services marketing is a fairly recent phenomenon in India and standards of excellence in this area can be attributed to the efforts of private sector players. This chapter outlines the path of one such player in the airline industry in India, Jet.

Jet Airways

Here we examine an example of a private sector airline company, Jet Airways, which entered the domestic segment in 1993 and has since become the favourite air carrier in India. The company brought in world class norms in professional service and efficiency that ranged from choice of modern aircraft to international training for its pilots and engineers, an accurate and efficient computerised reservation system, quick delivery of baggage on arrival at destination, and superior quality of in-flight food and refreshments. The marked difference compared to Indian public sector carrier Indian Airlines became quickly apparent to harried business travellers (Rajan, 2002).

Company mission
Jet Airways set for itself the mission of being the most preferred airline in India and to be the automatic first choice carrier for the travelling public. To quote Naresh Goyal, the entrepreneur who started Jet Airways: 'I always believed that India could come up with its own international quality airline. We have the talent, the enterprise and the skills.' They are also proud of their in-flight services:

- passengers get a 'hot meal' on all flights (cold meals were tried on short routes of 40 minutes or less but this was changed when the feedback from the Indian public did not favour cold meals)

- hot towels given before a meal, presumably to cater to the Indian habit of eating by hand rather than a fork and spoon

■ children are given a complimentary amusement kit

■ attentive crew and an environment of 'efficient informality'

Within three months of its launch Jet Airways acquired membership of the International Air Traffic Association (IATA) and has subsequently won several awards, including the distinction of being the first Indian airline to receive the World Travel Market Global Award.

Each of the preceding companies has been highly successful in becoming marketing-driven. The HLL case is as one would expect as it is a subsidiary of a multinational giant that is world-renowned for its marketing. The other companies likewise are leading examples of the marketing concept being adopted and utilised, with clear rewards in evidence from the marketplace. We believe these companies epitomise a movement beyond rhetoric to actual marketplace behaviour (i.e., the reality of marketing). We now turn to some examples of marketing mishaps, surprisingly often from firms one would expect to know better.

From marketing realities to marketing as a form of rhetoric

Readers may well be surprised by some of the examples that follow. Plainly, entry into a foreign market is not just a matter of offering whatever may suit the home market on the grounds there will be some sales. Instead, entrants need to explore the dynamics of markets they wish to serve, and then design marketing mixes that will satisfy customer needs. Anything less than this reveals proclaimed marketing orientation as a hollow sham, the equivalent perhaps of dressing a voracious wolf in innocuous clothing.

Kellogg's

Here there was an overestimation of demand, driven by an overoptimistic expectation by Kellogg's that consumers would give up their age-old traditional Indian homemade hot breakfast to switch instantly to the convenience of an expensive Kellogg breakfast cereal. In the initial phase of their launch in the Indian market in the 1990s the company displayed a complete lack of understanding of

Indian breakfast preferences and failed to realise that only a very small section of Indians who had been exposed to Western influences would be regular buyers of Kellogg's cereals. The company has since re-learnt a number of significant lessons and bounced back with a strategy to target its admittedly small base of core consumers with a range of products for adults and children.

Let us take a closer look at the factors involved in Kellogg's dismal performance in the first few years. Most multinational corporations who flocked to post-liberalisation India in the 1990s, were attracted by the 250 million strong Indian middle class projected by global consultancy firms. Eventually, most firms realised that this market was smaller, perhaps about 100–150 million urban residents, since most of the rural market was literally out of reach (still a huge market potential). And this 100–150 million was an estimate, largely for mass-market products. For premium-price products the market was actually tiny in comparison.

In the case of Kellogg's, besides overestimation, the second problem was overoptimism that Indian eating habits could be modified. Third, prices set were out of reach of average Indians at almost double the price of locally available cereal brands.

The brand, however, was of superior quality and had a strong differentiator in its extra crisp, thicker flakes compared to local players. This fact helped generate initial trials. Yet there were many other hurdles which Kellogg's did not anticipate. Despite offering a thicker and crisper flake, Indians were unused to the concept of cold milk. Instead they used hot milk which made the flakes soggy. Consumers who had purchased Kellogg's once at high prices did not return for a second helping.

The above facts illustrate how the wrong notions about the market when a multinational enters India can lead to a rocky start when realities turn out to be very different from company expectations. Here we have an example of a multinational that did not really understand the dynamics of the market. What Kellogg's actually did was make the assumption that consumers could be persuaded to buy. In essence, this highly successful multinational had returned in the Indian market to a previous stage of its development, sometimes referred to as 'sales orientation', an orientation seen now as a form of marketing rhetoric inevitably focused on company need to converts products into cash, and not necessarily to satisfy needs.

Pond's

Here is an example of a company that did not fully understand the equity of their brand name in the market. It is another interesting, smaller and yet significant case of failure which pertains to the company's experiment with categories other than women's cosmetics. Pond's is a well known brand in cosmetics. In 1993, a toothpaste and a baby product were launched under the Pond's name. The basic assumption was that the Pond's brand name and logo was so strong that it could be extended to other products. In the case of toothpastes, the company spoke of fresh breath and healthy teeth in their communication. While it was the right proposition, Pond's was not offering anything different from existing players in the toothpaste category and brand sales did not take off. Moreover, the association of the Pond's name with a cold cream for cosmetic purposes does not lend itself readily to being used for dental cleansing, or for babies. Again, what is happening here is an example of marketing arrogance, the assumption that consumers do not make connections between specific brand and product categories. Following category withdrawals, Ponds subsequently stuck to women's cosmetics.

Dettol

This brand provides another similar instance in not understanding the equity of their brand name in the market. When Dettol initially launched their soap brand in India there was an attempt to position it as beauty soap. This failed to enthuse the market since the brand's equity lies in germ fighting through the well-established Dettol antiseptic liquid. The soap brand had to be subsequently re-positioned as a germ fighter.

Summary

With the examples of Kellogg's, Pond's and Dettol we can see perhaps the flip side of the positive marketing experiences shared by the previous range of companies. In these three examples, the companies failed to take into consideration customer needs and market dynamics, or failed to understand the positive virtues of powerful brand equities which could have been damaged by misplaced brand extensions.

The point is, of course, that what these firms called 'marketing' (at least insofar as these examples are concerned) was nothing more than a form of rhetoric or wordplay, where no real attempt was made to understand – or, indeed, seek to satisfy – customer needs. Even more importantly, the marketing practised was in a sense a throwback to a world of marketing that was criticised and condemned even back in the 1960s. Perhaps more painfully obvious is that the firms practising marketing here are regarded as examples par excellence in their home nations. Hmmm! There are some serious issues to ponder here. Let us now turn to our penultimate section where trends associated with the rhetoric/reality construct are discussed.

Illustrative trends of the rhetoric/reality construct in the context of the Four Ps of the marketing mix

Let us understand development of the marketing concept in the Indian context through a broad look at the 4Ps.

Product

There have been several incidences where the business organisation had to adapt or modify the product form in order to compete in the Indian market. Suzuki had to provide extra ground clearance to suit Indian road conditions in its 'Swift' passenger car and renamed it 'Esteem' when it was launched in India.

Throughout the world PepsiCo is known as a soft drink company as well as a snacks company. Some of its snack brands (Ruffles, Cheetos, Hostess) are very successful internationally. The snack food division of the company, one of the early entrants in India, expected that these brands would perform equally well there. But, in 1994, the company withdrew Cheetos and Hostess due to insufficient volume sales. Ruffles was to be re-launched with more spicy flavours. Needless to say, this remaining brand did not do enough to sustain the entire division on its own. The company felt that unlike developed countries, the Indian market was not hugely bothered about the snack's form; in India taste is the predominant purchase motivator. In addition to that, crisps are perceived as a junk food by an average Indian. A more popular form of snack across all age groups in India is *namkeen* (dry savoury) based on traditional recipes. The market for that is estimated to be about 3,000,000 tonnes per annum. The product form allows itself to be scooped out or poured cleanly from the pack on to a palm for consumption, which cannot be done with crisps. In 1995 the company started marketing a variety of *namkeens* under its brand name 'Lehar' and avoided highlighting the 'Pepsi' name on the packaging in and around Delhi. By 1996, the brand sold 1,200 tonnes: a small player admittedly, but with significant growth opportunities.

The beverage division of the company also had to get more Indianised by adding a mango flavour (a very popular flavour in India) to its line of soft drinks under the brand name 'Slice'. PepsiCo is not marketing this flavour of soft drink elsewhere in the world.

Branding commodities

The attempt has been to expand the market by redefining competition to include the unorganised sector. In several categories, the unorganised sector accounts for a large section of buyer purchases, such as traditional purchases made through small neighbourhood grocers. Cooking oil has been branded for many decades and recent categories in commodity branding are salt and wheat. The strategy is to connote quality and purity through branding and packaging. In fact Nirma has a branded salt named *shudh* which literally means 'pure' in Hindi. Besides multinationals such as HLL and Pillsbury, several store brands have emerged as department stores launch their own labels of branded packaged commodities.

After-sales service

One area where the rhetoric did not really meet up with consumer expectations was after-sales service for consumer durables. But, from the mid-1990s onwards, growing competition has ensured that companies are brushing up in this area, where previously there was a lackadaisical approach.

Pricing

While the large middle-class consuming segment goes in for monthly purchases, a recent trend has been the introduction of low-unit, low-price pack sizes. The strategy has been to drive penetration in low and lower-middle income households and rural areas with low cost sachets and paise (Indian coin) packs. The pioneer here (as mentioned earlier) was a local regional player in shampoos, and today well over 50 per cent of the shampoo category volume comes from sachets. The 'smaller unit size = mass market' connotation has been firmly established with even toothpaste, chocolates and soft drinks going down this route in recent years to increase usage as well as expand the consumer base.

Even direct-selling cosmetic companies such as Avon, Oriflamme and Modicare, which draw their clientele from the top end, have changed track to launch product packs at reasonable price points to target a broader section of users. These companies, which earlier donned the premium tag, are increasingly launching trial packs and smaller packs to entice buyers. In fact, for the first time in any market in the world, Amway has launched shampoo and conditioner sachets.

To quote Samir Modi, managing director of Modicare India, in *The Economic Times* (a business newspaper):

> Smaller trial packets enabled the companies to get the customer to try the product and then move on to the bigger packs. As an Indian company, we have always believed that the value-for-money strategy is the best for the price-sensitive Indian customer. The foreign companies are now being forced to offer more realistically-priced products for the Indian markets.

Promotion or marketing communication

The advertising industry has come a long way from mere translations of English copy to local languages, to employing copywriters who can actually 'think' and write in the local language. This makes a world of difference when building local idiom and colloquial terminology into advertising copy. The use of 'Hinglish', a word coined for copy that combines English words with Hindi words, gained popularity in the 1990s and is here to stay. To cite an example: Pepsi's tag line, 'Ask For More', roughly translates to 'Yeh Dil Mange More' in 'Hinglish' (*Yeh Dil Mange* are Hindi words spelt in English in the ad and combined with the English word 'more').

In line with the Indian craze for song and dance in films, most of the television and radio advertising is jingle-based with catchy hummable tunes that re-play in the consumer's mind for greater recall of brand. Television is by far the widest-reaching medium in the country and many an Indian brand has been built on the power of this medium.

Another trend is cause-related marketing which is gaining ground in India. Brand associations provide a platform for the company's position on social and environmental issues and are carefully selected to cue a fit with the company's main business areas. Below are some examples:

- Maruti Udyog, the largest car manufacturer, has associated itself with environment trends with air pollution campaigns and pollution checking counters.

- Kellogg's contributes towards creating awareness on the ill effects of iron deficiency

- MRF Tyres have espoused the cause of promoting stress-free driving on roads with an ingenious idea that talks about the value of the 'smile'

- Tata Steel contributes towards creating more healthcare centres in small towns and villages

- cosmetics MNC Avon makes a gesture towards creating awareness about breast cancer, while Amway supports the National Project for the Blind

- there has been a computer literacy drive by NIIT, a computer software education company

At times, an organisation planning to diversify or launch new products also takes the 'social' route. For instance, when J&J launched its new Vision Product division, which sells Acuvue and Vistavue brands of disposable contact lenses, the company decided to donate a percentage of its sales proceeds to eye-care societies. Cause-related emotions play a key role in creating involvement and bonding between consumers and the brand.

Initiatives in distribution

Distribution is being increasing streamlined with information technology based initiatives, such as the following:

1   HLL: establishment of a satellite-based voice and data communication network which links over 200 locations all over the country including the head office, branch offices, factories, depots and key distribution stockists.

2   National Dairy Development Board: a government body involved in milk production plans to use IT to connect on-line Gujarat's 12 cooperative milk dairies with their marketing arm, GCMMF, their depots and key dealers.

3   BPL: the company is striving to bring down delivery lead times. The aim is to have the actual production programming work in more or less perfect conjunction with inputs from the various markets it operates in. All BPL dealers are now linked via nodes, ensuring on-line availability of information on inventory status and sales movement. The production facilities are linked to the supply chain with near-fresh demand data.

Summary and conclusion

We have seen product upgrading, product improvements and brand extensions to the Clinic range, the need for distinctiveness among youth tapped by Close-Up toothpaste, the evolution of Lifebuoy, the unique concept in Fair & Lovely, the transformation of an industry by Titan, the right pricing for the mass market by Amul, the impeccable service standards of Jet Airways, and so forth. We have also seen the dangers of not fully understanding the Indian consumer, as in Kellogg's initial failure.

Based on these examples, let us pick out some of the marketing prerequisites that emerge and highlight common threads that run through the several examples cited in this chapter.

1   Here, as elsewhere in the world, companies have to take into consideration the needs, wants, and desires of target markets, and then deliver desired satisfactions more effectively and efficiently than the competition.

2   It is not enough simply to offer un-adapted products and services to customers, by relying on the mistaken assumption that what works at home will also work here.

3   A clear lesson here is that marketing cannot be applied once and then forgotten! Instead the process of marketing, *analysis, planning, implementation, and control*, must become literally that: *an ongoing interactive market-driven process that permeates deeply the mindset and culture of an organisation.*

4   How can this work? We suggest that marketing must involve:

(a)   a commitment to R&D constantly to upgrade, improve products and offer new products;

(b)   presence across the segments: a trend towards companies catering to different price points, in order to widen the consumer base for their products;

(c)   understanding Indian traditions, habits, behaviour and lifestyle (e.g., food habits as seen in the Kellogg's and Jet Airways case, skin care needs, hair grooming needs, price–value equations, etc.);

(d)   a clear-cut strategy to iron out distribution bottlenecks and speed up the process of order and supply with the use of IT;

(e)   rural initiatives if marketing a mass brand. There is a large and adequate urban market size available. In fact the size of the Indian urban market is equivalent in size to the entire US population. However, post-entry and growth in the urban market, for a marketer looking to expand and re-enter the growth phase, especially in mature categories, tapping the rural area is the only way to expand the market;

(f)   a commitment to quality: as seen in the cases of BPL and Jet Airways, quality today is multidimensional and ranges from product orientation to customer orientation to process orientation with the tightest control over delivery lead times and management of supply;

(g)   understanding the power of advertising and communication in brand building and an investment in this area as a planned on-going activity.

Without these factors in place, no matter how large, diverse and profitable a company may be, it will fail. Oh, it may well offer 'marketing', but it will be seen as no more than a rhetorical device, and not as a deeply-held organisational philosophy which applies everywhere, and to everyone.

Appendix 9.1: Understanding Rural India

Some 72.21 per cent of Indians live in rural areas and it is therefore important to understand what rural means. To give a simple definition, a rural area is one where a majority of the population is engaged in agricultural activities and the village has a self-governing council called the *panchayat* rather than the municipality or corporation that governs an urban settlement.

There are around 5,80,000 villages in India. A typical Indian village will have a population anywhere from 500 to 2,000 and will not have a motorable approach road leading into it but rather a loosely defined mud path. To reach the nearest bus stop to an urban centre means a 3–4 km walk for a rural dweller. Most of the dwellings in the village will have a single room with a thatched roof and hand-made brick/mud walls. Larger villages will have a few proper constructions that house a post office, health centre or school. In most villages there is a small temple at the entrance to the village.

Rural electrification is very high but even today an estimated 10–15 per cent of villages still await electrification. At the household level, at least one out of every three rural homes has electricity. In many villages there is now at least one television set, usually owned by the village headman, and it is a common sight to see a large crowd gathered around the set at dusk to watch a weekend movie.

Appendix 9.2: Generation Next

A global MTV study, 'Sources of Cool', was conducted among youth by a leading independent brand consultancy, Sterling Group. The research was done across 15 cities worldwide: researchers visited their bedrooms, their homes, asked them about their likes and dislikes, visited their clubs and discos to see what was cool, observed what youth were wearing, the words they used and so on.

Insights on Indian youth from the study included the following:

- there is huge appetite for the new among Indian youth in Mumbai
- they have an insatiable desire to be first
- there is a strong culture, so they don't have to borrow from other cultures (they are therefore much more selective in what they take from the world)
- they have their 'eyes wide open'
- city youth have similar attitudes whether they are from Mumbai, Tokyo or London (you can put a youth from Mumbai in Buenos Aires or in New York and he will feel pretty comfortable); but in smaller towns, they are very diverse.

Another study on Indian youth conducted by MTV India revealed the following: symbols of success include money, Hrithik (a 21 year old Hindi movie box office draw), Sachin (world renowned cricketer) and Cyrus Broacha (an MTV VJ who can tickle anybody's funny bone). Atal Behari Vajpayee (the current Indian Prime Minister) is their coolest politician and Sonu Nigam (a singer of Hindi pop music) is their coolest singer.

Source: www.briefonline.com interview (in 2001) with Simon Williams, Chairman, Sterling Group.

Chapter
Drawing the strands together

philip j. kitchen

Introduction

This book has considered 'marketing' in eight nation states around the world. In each country, contributors have explored the 'rhetoric' and reality of marketing by, among other things, comparing two case studies. It seems evident that there is tremendous variability in terms of the application of the marketing concept not only *between* industrial and industrialising nations but also *within* different firms and even within the same country. In this final chapter we explore the following questions, as anticipated in Chapter 1:

1 Is there a difference between proclaimed adherence, and allegiance, to the marketing concept in developing and developed nations?

2 Are customer needs satisfied by the products and services offered by businesses in countries at different stages of economic development?

3 Are the stages of economic development approach a 'red herring' when considering how firms actually *apply* the marketing concept?

4 Is there a difference between what the marketing rhetoric promises versus what is actually delivered: that is, the reality?

5 If there is a difference between rhetoric and reality, where does this difference lie?

6 How does this affect overall marketing performance?

7   What effect might a pronounced gap between rhetoric and reality
     have:
     (a)   on consumers?
     (b)   on distributors?
     (c)   on competitors?
     (d)   on other publics?
     (e)   on the organisation itself?

We preface discussion of these question with an analysis of what the
marketing rhetoric/reality construct actually means. We then consider the case examples using each side of the construct. Then the
above questions are discussed. Finally, a critical conclusion is
offered.

The marketing rhetoric/reality construct

The marketing rhetoric/reality construct was taken to be a qualitative
measure of whether companies operating in different nation
states utilised marketing *either* as a form of rhetoric *or* as a realistic
device to drive the philosophy deep into an organisational culture
resulting in exchanges satisfying both to consumers and customers
and to the organisation in terms of sales, profits, market share
and so forth. It is arguable that industrially advanced nations have
populations that are perceived to be relatively sophisticated in relation
to purchase and consumption decisions. It can also be argued that, for
many of these firms, the way marketing is practised *at home* is also
the way it is practised in other nation-states around the world. As seen
in Chapter 1, however, the world cannot be neatly divided into developed and developing nations. Today, the world is characterised by
interdependence, where many multinational and global corporations
compete throughout the world and in many nation states.

   In this scenario, the American model of marketing is taken to be
applicable to all nation states, and to firms operating within its
boundaries; but is it? Again and again, we return to the issue or question of just what is marketing intended to be: is it really an organisational philosophy that attempts to balance organisational and
consumer needs? Can it be translated or, put another way, *applied* in
such a way as to produce appropriate outcomes? The answer is, of

course, both 'yes' and 'no': yes, in the sense that if applied it does result in appropriate outcomes, but firms can and do apparently succeed without the assistance of the marketing concept, save only in a rhetorical form.

It is wrong for academics and practitioners to assume that the American model of marketing, as set forth valiantly in so many texts, is actually applicable in other countries. For many businesses and firms elsewhere, the application of marketing – ostensibly in the name of customers and consumers – of benefits they may, and often do not, receive is no more than a rhetorical device. In business after business and industry after industry, apparent consumer innovations are introduced which annoy, confuse, and irritate customers. They are in fact no more than organisational innovations designed to create organisational efficiencies by keeping customers – the life-blood of the organisation – at a distance. Very few organisations are really interested in the customers whose needs they claim to serve. It is only when organisational inefficiencies are clearly recognisable by customers, who then take their patronage elsewhere, that businesses may start to take marketing rather more seriously. And this would also be true when extending the marketing concept into non-profit areas, such as politics, when even hardened rhetorical political experts decide a change is needed to attract voters. In the political sphere, however, what passes for marketing is so pure a form of rhetoric as to be almost undiluted.

Yet there is a still deeper argument. Marketing itself, as currently defined, may be no more than a form of rhetoric. Marketing texts rightly applaud businesses that have been successful in meeting marketplace needs. But do those businesses meet those needs because they have applied 'marketing', or because they have temporarily connected with real, identifiable needs? Marketing itself may well be no more than a form of *ex post facto* rationalisation in terms of businesses that are successful: the business is successful, ergo it must be practising the marketing concept. The literature fails to explain why successful businesses often, after having created exchanges successfully, then engage in a process of product and service dilution, which undoubtedly does increase profits but may damage the business in the long term. Thus, a more cynical and perhaps realistic model of marketing may be to say that the organisation does all of the following:

1   It creates successful products and services that do satisfy needs (at this stage, something resembling the marketing reality construct may be clearly recognisable).

2   It facilitates market-leadership position (still in a marketing reality stage, but marketing authors around the world are quick to acknowledge the company as 'market-driven' or 'marketing orientated').

3   It begins the process of breaking down every component of the product or service and its marketing to extract the last ounce of profit (note this process continues year on year throughout the life of the product or service), simultaneously seeking to continually lower costs of production. (Here the marketing reality construct is abandoned in favour of market image; unfortunately for customers and consumers, marketing has already moved a long way down the track to being no more than a form of rhetoric.)

4   It aims to provide consumers with as little as possible for the maximum amount of profitability: that is, the aim is to satisfy psychological rather than the original functional benefits. (This may work for a long time as customers fail to recognise that their needs are not met, and that the organisation is saying one thing, but doing another.)

5   It assumes there is little or no relationship between what the organisation does (i.e., its behaviour), and the brands it sells (again – and this is still a form of marketing rhetoric – the problem may be that many organisations may start genuinely to believe that what they offer customers is in and for their benefit, rather than the other way round).

The end result of this process is a form of marketing that is organisationally-oriented rather than consumer- or customer-oriented. Such marketing does allow organisations to openly proclaim allegiance to the marketing concept, and simultaneously could help explain why so many organisations appear to be (and actually are) incompetent in marketing terms. Thus, in many so-called 'mature markets', there is still scope for market entry and growth by applying marketing in a realistic manner. The problem for market entry 'wannabes' is identifying in a persuasive way just what existing players are doing that is frankly inimical to consumer interests.

The case examples

In the eight chapters covering nation-states in this book, there are examples of businesses that practise marketing in a realistic way. These firms explore market dynamics and adjust marketing mixes, sometimes redesigning and repositioning products and services to make them more applicable and meaningful to customers and consumers. They act in societally acceptable ways. They are good corporate citizens. They reap the rewards of buyer behaviour from consumers and customers who are brand loyal, who allow the firm the privilege of creating exchanges on an on-going basis. There is, of course, no guarantee that today's successful organisations may not turn into tomorrow's rhetoricians.

However, there are also examples of businesses for whom marketing is no more than a form of rhetoric. Moreover, it is possible for a company to practise marketing in a realistic manner *in some markets*, whilst in other markets, businesses offer what they have *with no real attempt* to satisfy consumer needs, all the while proclaiming ostensible consumer innovations which are in fact designed to create greater profitability. Or, alternatively, many businesses simply continue to offer the same products in similar ways while the quest to wrest profitability continues at the expense of consumers. The cases imply that rather than businesses moving from production, product, sales, and marketing orientations over time in a progressive manner, they simply apply the most appropriate orientation *to them* differentially as needed.

Critical questions

1 Is there a difference between proclaimed adherence, and allegiance, to the marketing concept in developing and developed nations?

The short answer is no, there appears to be no substantive difference in nations at different stages of economic development. Admittedly, the concept may have taken longer to take root in management thinking and practice, but this can be laid at the door of general economic and social development, which are in turn affected by cultural, national, militaristic and political factors. It may be argued, however, that marketing can be (and is) applied differentially using the rhetoric and reality construct. Despite the existence of businesses for whom marketing is a reality, it is my view that for most firms, marketing will never be more than a rhetorical device. Thus it would seem high time in many countries around the world, for those teaching marketing, that a study of what marketing is, and how it can be applied should be available. The American model of marketing, for so long taught apparently as if it were an article of faith, needs to be analysed and re-worked in a more appropriate form for different national contexts.

2 Are customer needs satisfied by the products and services offered by businesses in countries at different stages of economic development?

The answer would appear to be in the affirmative. However, this may be purely a function of product availability until better alternatives become available. There seems little doubt that marketing can be applied differentially in different countries based on stages of development theory, but there is also evidence of significant consumer sophistication. Failure to apply the marketing concept in full may mean an inability to penetrate that market. Note that failure here would in fact be a failure of management to apply the marketing concept.

*3 Are the stages of economic development approach a 'red herring', when considering how firms actually **apply** the marketing concept?*

Evidence suggests that the stages of economic development approach is of value and significance in terms of applying marketing *initially*. An approach may be countenanced where a focus on sales orientation, or even production, may be appropriate in the short to medium term. But as markets or their customers become more mature and sophisticated it seems inappropriate to continue to offer unadapted, unaltered products as if consumers in the market were the same as consumers elsewhere. Thus the old hoary argument of adaptation versus differentiation should not depend as it does on corporate strategy, but upon market dynamics.

4 Is there a difference between what the marketing rhetoric promises versus what is actually delivered: that is, the reality?

As discussed previously, there is a substantial difference. As argued, it does not take any great analysis or understanding to perceive that, for most organisations, marketing will never be more than a form of rhetoric. There is a very great need to consider marketing from specific country perspectives. Widespread dissemination of the American model (i.e., via teaching) does not mean widespread dissemination of the marketing concept in a realistic sense. Of course, it might be that the American model of marketing is only applicable *in America*. Certainly, there are strong grounds for suspecting that what is proclaimed as consumer orientation is in fact no more and no less than organisational orientation dressed in new trendy clothes, high heels, and given a high-pitched marketing voice. There is a nagging and recurrent suspicion that not only are most businesses incompetent in terms of marketing, but they have little real desire to understand what creates and maintains customer loyalty. Indeed I would go so far as to say that many firms, by their own actions and behaviours (or lack of these), deliberately annoy, confuse and irritate the very customers they were intended to serve. Students of marketing in virtually every country (bar perhaps the USA), are surrounded by, immersed in and maybe even inured to organisations who are prima facie examples of marketing and managerial incompetence, as seen by customers.

5 If there is a difference between rhetoric and reality, where does this difference lie?

The difference lies in managerial ability and the application of resources to explore the dynamics of the markets in which they compete. The result will be that when more satisfying offers are made, and perhaps when consumer irritations peak, the lack of marketing orientation will result in declining sales, declining profits, and decline in market share and stock market values. These companies will blame market dynamics, when really it is they who have failed to understand and adapt to market dynamics.

6 How does this affect overall marketing performance?

Most businesses regularly underperform in terms of what marketing promises versus what is delivered. Business fail to apply marketing reality and imagine that markets will never tell the difference between rhetoric and reality and fail to deliver consistent value.

7 What effect might a pronounced gap between rhetoric and reality have?

Any identifiable gaps between what is promised and what and how benefits are delivered will impact on virtually every level in terms of distribution. Moreover, such a gap opens the door to competitive forces. Ultimately, it also means that the organisation is less efficient that it might otherwise be. Consumer sales and loyalties are the ultimate life blood of the organisation. They are ignored or treated lightly at the organisation's peril.

Summary and conclusion

Perhaps it is too much to analyse marketing from the perspective of how and in what ways it might be applied? Perhaps it is too much to assume that what is taught to student via the (US-dominated) literature would have little resonance for some businesses in the real world, despite 30–40 years of such tuition? Maybe the marketing concept is *either* a managerial philosophy that can be learned and applied in a realistic manner, *or* can be used by companies purely as a rhetorical device? Perhaps, as customers and consumers gain more knowledge and information about the way marketing *works*, or is supposed to work, they may perceive an imbalance between what is done ostensibly in their names and for their benefit, versus what is actually received? Maybe a re-examination of what marketing *is* now is needed. Certainly, in this short text, we have many examples of marketing reality versus marketing rhetoric. For readers, it may be worth asking: where do they stand? And, moreover, does it make a difference to the ways we act, either as a business or as a consumer? Food for thought?

Bibliography

Acland, A. (2001) 'Ruling Puts DM Industry Firmly on Back Foot', *Marketing Direct*, December, p. 3.

A.C. Nielsen (2001) *Television Audience Share in New Zealand*. www.acnielsen. co.nz. Accessed 4 July 2001.

Alderson, W. (1958) 'The Analytical Framework for Marketing', *Conference of Marketing Teachers*, University of California; pp.15–28.

Alderson, W. (1964) 'A Normative Theory of Marketing Systems', in Cox *et al.*, p.101.

Anonymous (1999) 'UK Perspectives Air Photographic Census', *Precision Marketing*, 24 May, p.5.

Arndt, J. (1976) 'The Marketing Thinking of Tomorrow: Beyond the Marketing Concept Toward New Dignity and Responsible Freedom for Managers and Consumers', *Working Paper*, Norwegian School of Economics and Business Administration, February.

Arnold, C. (2002) reported by E. Rubach 'Up Close and Too Personal', *Precision Marketing*, 1 February, p.12.

Baker, M. (ed.) (1999) 'The Future of Marketing', in *Encyclopaedia of Marketing*, International Thomson Press, London; pp.816–31.

Band, W.A. (1991) *Creating Value for Customers: Designing and Implementing a Total Corporate Strategy*, John Wiley, New York.

Barton, C. (2001a) 'Animators Hole Out with TV Golf Deal', *NZ Herald*, 22 June, On-line edition www.nzherald.co.nz. Accessed 22 July 2001.

Barton, C. (2001b) 'Virtual Spectator Serves up a Smorgasbord of New Media', *NZ Herald*, 24 November, On-line edition www.nzherald.co.nz. Accessed 18 February 2002.

Bateson, J.E.G. and Hoffman, K.D. (1999) *Managing Services Marketing*, 4th edn, The Dryden Press, Fort Worth, TX.

Bell, J., Demick, D., Ibbotson, P., Karajan, S. and Wood, V. (1997) 'Marketing Education without Borders: Exploiting New Information Technologies', *Journal of Marketing Management*, Vol. 13, No. 6, pp.615–24.

Berry, L.L. (1981) 'The Employee as a Customer', *Journal of Retail Banking*, Vol. 3, No. 1, pp.33–40.

Blagoev, V. (1984a) 'Risk Factors in the Innovation of Machine-Tools for Export to the Third World Markets', *Proceedings of the Conference on Marketing of Machine-Tools, Electronics and Equipment for the Third World Markets*, Sofia, pp.34–7.

Blagoev, V. (1984b) 'The Problems of Quality and Competitiveness of Exported Machine-Tools', *Journal of Foreign Trade*, No. 3, pp.2–6.

Blagoev, V. (1988) *Marketing in Definitions and Examples*, 2nd edn 1989, Dr P. Beron Ltd, Sofia.

Blagoev, V. (1998) *Marketing*, 1st edn, Vecco, Sofia.

Blagoev, V., Kirkov, H. and Milanova, M. (1986) *The Role of Marketing in Innovation Management*, BCCI, Sofia.

Borch, F.J. (1957) *The Marketing Philosophy as a Way of Business Life*, General Electric, New York.

Borna, S. and Avila, S. (1999) 'Genetic Information: Consumers' Right to Privacy Versus Insurance Companies' Right to Know: A Public Opinion Surveys', *Journal of Business Ethics*, Vol. 19, No. 3, pp.355–62.

Boyter, G. (2002) reported in D. Reed 'Dunn Humby Spices up Direct Marketing with Cinnamon', European Centre for Customer Strategies, February, http://www.eccs.uk.com/crm or www.eccs.uk.com/crm

Bozduganov, A., Obreshkova, M., Blagoev, V., Kirkov, H. and Monev, S. (1984) *Marketing Management in R&D Organizations and Foreign Trade Companies*, BCCI, Sofia.

Brooks, D. (2000) *Bobos in Paradise*, Simon & Schuster, New York.

Brown, S. (1999) 'Postmodernism: The End of Marketing?', in D. Brownlie, M. Saren, R. Wensley and R. Whittington (1999) *Rethinking Marketing*, Sage, London.

Brown, S. (2000) *Postmodern Marketing Two: Telling Tales*, International Thomson Business, London.

Carson, C.D. (1999) 'What it takes and where to get it', *Working Paper*, University of North Carolina.

Caruana, A. and Calleya, P. (1998) 'The Effect of Internal Marketing on Organisational Commitment among Retail Bank Managers', *International Journal of Bank Marketing*, Vol. 16, No. 3, pp.108–16.

Chae, S.I. (1985) 'A Study of Marketing Title and Unification', *The Korean Academy of Business Histories*, Vol. 4, No. 1, pp.1–22.

Channel 4 (1990) Direct Marketing. Equinox Series.

Chetty, S.K. and Hamilton, R.T. (1996) 'The Process of Exporting in Owner-Controlled Firms', *International Small Business Journal*, Vol. 14, No. 2, pp.12–25.

Ciampa, D. (1992) *Total Quality: A User's Guide for Implementation*, Addison-Wesley, Reading, MA.

CIM (2001) The Impact of E-Business on Marketing and Marketers, October, Cookham. Website for CIM Direct purchase: http://www.connectedinmarketin.co.uk, tel. 44 (0) 1628 427427.

Clegg, A. (2001) 'Strong Medicine', *Database Marketing*, March, pp.14–20

Clifton, L. (2001) Personal correspondence with Executive Director, Communication Agencies Association of New Zealand, July 2001.

Compton, F., George, W.R., Gronroos, C. and Karvinen, M. (1987) 'Internal Marketing', in J.A. Czepiel, C.A. Congram and J. Shanahan (eds), *The Services Challenge: Integrating for Competitive Advantage*, Proceedings of the 5th Annual Services Marketing Conference, American Marketing Association, Chicago; pp.7–12.

Cova, B. (1999) 'From Marketing to Societing', in Brownlie *et al.* (1999) *Rethinking Marketing*, Sage, London.

Cowell, D.W. (1984) *The Marketing of Services*, Butterworth-Heinemann, London.

Cox, R., Alderson, W. and Shapiro, S. (eds) (1964) *Theory in Marketing*, Richard D. Irwin, Homewood, Il.

Day, G.S. and Wensley, R. (1983) 'Marketing Theory with a Strategic Orientation', *Journal of Marketing*, Vol. 47 (Fall), pp.101–10.

Dholakia, N. and Arndt, J. (eds) (1985) *Changing the Course of Marketing: Alternative Paradigms for Widening Marketing Theory*, JAI Press, Greenwich, CT.

Dibb, S. (2001) 'New Millennium, New Segments: Moving Towards the Segment of One?', *Journal of Strategic Marketing*, Vol. 9, No. 3 (Summer), pp.193–214.

Dickson, I (1993) 'From Chumps to Champs', *Euromoney*, January, p.85.

Doganov, D. (1998) *Marketing in Tourism*, Princeps, Sofia.

Doganov, D. and Malamin, T. (1983) *The Catalogue as an Instrument of the Contemporary Marketing*, BCCI, Sofia.

Doganov, D. and Radoicheva, R. (1984) *Advertising Research in the Foreign Trade Relations*, BCCI, Sofia.

Doganov, D. and Radoicheva, R. (1987) *Advertising in the Foreign Trade*, BCCI, Sofia.

Drake, O.B. (2001) Speech from AAAA President and CEO at the General Session of the AAAA Management Committee in Naples, Florida, 19 April. www.aaaa.org/transcripts. Accessed 10 July 2001.

Eagle, L.C., Hyde, K.F., Fourie, W.A., Padisetti, M.V. and Kitchen, P.J. (1999) 'Perceptions of Integrated Marketing Communications among Marketers and Advertising Agency Executives in New Zealand', *International Journal of Advertising*, Vol. 18, No. 1, pp.89–120.

Ein-dor, P., Myers, M.D. and Raman, K.S. (1997) 'Information Technology in Three Small Developed Countries', *Journal of Management Information Systems*, Vol. 13, No. 4, pp.61–89.

Eiseley, L. (1978) *The Star Thrower*, Times Books, New York; p.99.

Evans, M., O'Malley, L. and Patterson, M. (2001) 'Bridging the Direct Marketing–Direct Consumer Gap: Some Solutions from Qualitative Research', *Qualitative Market Research: An International Journal*, Vol. 4, No. 1, pp.17–24.

Fisk, R.P., Brown, S.W. and Bitner, M. (1993) 'Tracking the Evolution of the Services Marketing Literature', *Journal of Retailing*, Vol. 69, No. 1, pp.61–103.

Firat, A.F., Dholakia, N. and Bagozzi, R.P. (eds) (1987) *Philosophical and Radical Thought in Marketing*, Lexington Books, Lexington, MA.

Flipo, J. (1986) 'Service Firms: Interdependence of External and Internal Marketing Strategies', *European Journal of Marketing*, Vol. 20, Part 8, pp.5–14.

Fong, K. (2000) 'IT Helps Banks to Build Good Customer Relationships', *The Star Business*, 22 May, p.11.

Fournier, S., Dobscha, S. and Mick, D.G. (1998) 'Preventing the Premature Death of Relationship Marketing', *Harvard Business Review*, January–February, pp.120–33.

France, E. (1998) as reported by S. Davies, 'New Data Privacy Storm Threatens Global Trade War', *Financial Mail on Sunday*, 29 March, p.3.

Fridenson, P. (1981) 'French Automobile Marketing, 1890–1979', in A. Okochi and K. Shimokawa, *Development of Mass Marketing*, University of Tokyo Press, Tokyo; pp.127–62.

Fullerton, R. (1987) 'The Poverty of Ahistorical Analysis: Present Weakness and Future Cure in U.S. Marketing Thought', in Firat *et al.* (1987).

Gaynor, B. (1999). 'Analysis: Filling Foreigners Pockets', *NZ Herald*, 2 October, On-line edition www.nzherald.co.nz. Accessed 4 July 2001.

George, W.R. (1990) 'Internal Marketing and Organisational Behaviour: a Partnership in Developing Customer-Conscious Employees at Every Level', *Journal of Business Research*, Vol. 20, No. 1 (January), pp.63–70.

George, W.R. and Gronroos, C. (1989) 'Developing Customer Conscious Employees at Every Level – Internal Marketing', in C.A. Congram and M.L. Friedman (eds), *Handbook of Services Marketing*, AMACOM, New York.

Gofton, K. (2001) 'Firms Fail to Relate to Customers', *Marketing Direct*, January, p.10.

Goldstar (1993) *Goldstar's 35 Years History: 1958–1993*, Goldstar.

Goldstar House Organ (1991) Vol. 5, p.3.

Grant, N. (2000) 'Real Progress For Virtual Spectator', *NZ Business*, March, p.9.

Gronroos, C. (1981a) 'Internal Marketing an Integral Part of Marketing Theory', in J.H. Donnelly and W.R. George (eds), *Marketing of Services, Proceedings of the American Marketing Association*, pp.236–8.

Gronroos, C. (1981b) 'Internal Marketing – Theory and Practice', *Proceedings of the American Marketing Association Services Marketing Conference*, pp.41–7.

Gronroos, C. (1984a) 'A Service Quality Model and its Marketing Implications', *European Journal of Marketing*, Vol. 18, No. 4, pp.36–44.

Gronroos, C. (1984b) *Strategic Management and Marketing in the Service Sector*, Lund. Student litterateur, cited in Groonroos (1985), op cit.

Gronroos, C. (1985) 'Internal Marketing: Theory and Practice', *Proceedings of the American Marketing Association*, Chicago; pp.41–7.

Gronroos, C. (2000) *Service Management and Marketing: A Customer Relationship Management Approach*, 2nd edn, Wiley, Chichester; p.331.

Gummesson, E. (2000) 'Internal marketing in the Light of Relationship Marketing and Network Organisations', in R.J. Varey and B.R. Lewis (eds), *Internal Marketing: Directions for Management*, Routledge, London; pp.27–42.

Haeckel (2001) in Mitchell (2001a).

Hanim Adnan (2001) 'Maybank Expects Better Results Next Quarter', *The Star Business*, 6 September, p.5.

Hansard (1999) *House of Commons Debates*, 3 February, p.22.

Health Funds Association (2002) Website http://www.healthfunds.org.nz. Accessed 26 February 2002.

Heskett, J.L., Jones, T.O., Loveman, G.W., Sasser Jr, W.E. and Schlesinger, L.A. (1994) 'Putting the service-profit chain to work', *Harvard Business Review*, March–April, pp.164–74.

Hetzel, P. (1996) 'The Fall and Rise of Marketing Fundamentalism: The Case of the "Nature & Découvertes" Distribution Concept', in S. Brown, J. Bell and D. Carson, *Marketing Apocalypse*, Routledge, London; pp.171–88.

Hetzel, P. (1998) 'The Current State of the Clothing Industry and Market in France', *Journal of Fashion Marketing and Management*, Vol. 2, No. 4, pp.386–91.

Hetzel, P. (1999) 'Gender Issues and New Product Development in the French Automotive Industry', *International Journal of New Product Development and Innovation Management*, Vol. 1, No. 3, pp.219–26.

Hetzel, P. (2000) 'Where are we Going? Perceptions of French Marketing Academics', *Journal of Marketing Management*, Vol. 16, No. 7, pp.697–716.

Holton, R.J. (1998) *Globalization and the Nation State*, St Martin's Press, New York.

Hristov, S. (1998) *Strategic Marketing*, Economy University Publishing Co., Sofia.

Hunt, S.D. (1983) 'General Theories and Fundamental Explanada of Marketing', *Journal of Marketing*, Vol. 47 (Fall), pp.9–17.

Hunt, S.D. (1991) *Modern Marketing Theory: Critical Issues in the Philosophy of Marketing Science*, Southwestern, Cincinnati, OH.

Hunt, S.D. (1992) 'Marketing is . . . .', *Journal of the Academy of Marketing Science*, Vol. 20, No. 4, pp.301–11.

Introna, L. and Powlouda, A. (1999) 'Privacy in the Information Age: Stakeholders, Interests and Values', *Journal of Business Ethics*, Vol. 22, No. 3, pp.27–38.

Irwin, J. (2001) Personal correspondence with Executive Director, Association of New Zealand Advertisers, July 2001.

Jelev, S. (1995) *Marketing Research*, Economy University Publishing Co., Sofia.

Jephcott, J. and Bock, T. (1998) 'The Application and Validation of Data Fusion', *Journal of the Market Research Society*, Vol. 40, No. 3, pp.185–205.

Judd, V.C. (1987) 'Differentiate with the 5th P: People', *Industrial Marketing Management*, Vol. 16, No. 4, pp.241–7.

Karakasheva, L. and Boeva, B. (1979) *Marketing Management in the Foreign Trade in the Capitalist Countries*, Economic University Graduate School, Sofia.

Karakasheva, L., Mencheva, L., and Markova, B. (1997) *Marketing*, Prizma, Sofia.

Kasper, H., Helsdingen, P.V. and Vries, W.D. (1999) *Services Marketing Management*, Wiley, Chichester; pp.443, 450.

Keegan, W.J. (1999) *Global Marketing Management*, 6th edn, Prentice-Hall, Englewood Cliffs, NJ; p.45.

Keegan, W.J. and Green, M.C. (1997) *Principles of Global Marketing*, Prentice-Hall, Englewood Cliffs, NJ; inside front cover.

Kelly, G.M. (1995) 'Structural Change in New Zealand: Some Implications For The Labour Market Regime' *International Labour Review*, Vol. 13, No. 4, pp.333–59.

Kennedy, P.D. (1999) *Europe and New Zealand – The New Millennium Beckons*. Presentation by Director, European Division, Ministry of Foreign Affairs and Trade at 'New Zealand and its Relations with Europe', Seminar, Waikato University, Hamilton.

Kennedy, R. and Ehrenberg, A. (2000) 'What's in a Brand?', *Research*, April, pp.30–2.

Keremidchiev, E. (1975) *Marketing – Complex Market Policy in the Export Markets*, BCCI, Sofia.

Keremidchiev, E. (1990) *Foundations of Marketing – Strategies, Management*, Vek 22, Sofia.

Key, A. (2000) 'The Taxman: Snooper or Helper?', *Marketing Direct*, February, p.13.

Kim, Linsu (2000) 'Management Research in Korea: A Call for Change', *Korea Management Review*, Vol. 29, No. 3, pp.293–314.

Kim, Y.J. *et al.* (1996) 'Analysis of Korea Marketing Journal: 1971–1998', *Marketing Journal*, Vol. 14, No. 2, pp.147–73.

King, R.L. (1965) 'The Marketing Concept', in G. Schwartz, *Science in Marketing*, Wiley, New York; pp.70–97.

Kirkov, H. and Blagoev, V. (1983) 'R&D and Contemporary Marketing', *IKO*, No. 8, Sofia, pp.66–7.

Kitchen, P.J. (ed.) (2003) *The Future of Marketing: Critical 21st-Century Perspectives*, Palgrave, Basingstoke.

Kitchen, P.J. and Eagle, L.C. (2001) 'Globalization, Integration and Gray Marketing: Marketing Communications in New Zealand', *Massey University, College of Business, Department of Commerce Working Paper Series*, 01.14.

Kitchen, P.J. and Schultz, D.E. (1998) 'IMC: A UK Ad Agency Perspective', *Journal of Marketing Management*, Vol. 14, No. 5, pp.465–85.

Kitchen, P.J. and Schultz, D.E. (1999) 'A Multi-Country Comparison of the Drive for Integrated Marketing Communications', *Journal of Advertising Research*, Vol. 39, No. 1, pp.1–17.

Kitchen, P.J. and Schultz, D.E. (eds) (2001) *Raising the Corporate Umbrella: Corporate Communications in the 21st Century*, Palgrave, Basingstoke.

Klassova, S., Ivanov, P., Stankovich, L., Stankova, L., Mladenova, G., Baleva, V., Naidenov, N., Vassileva, L., Durankev, B. and Gerov, A. (1999) *Introduction to Marketing*, Economy University Publishing Co., Sofia.

Kohli, K. and Jaworski, B. (1990) 'Market Orientation: The Construct, Research Propositions, and Managerial Implications', *Journal of Marketing*, Vol. 54, pp.1–58.

Koshy, A. and Sinha, S. (1999), 'Amul' (A case study), Indian Institute of Management, Ahmedabad (IIMA).

Kotler, P. (1986) 'Megamarketing', *Harvard Business Review*, Vol. 64, No. 2 (March/April), pp.117–24.

Kotler, P. (1997) *Marketing Management: Analysis, Planning, Implementation, and Control*. 9th edn, Prentice-Hall International, Englewood Cliffs, NJ, pp.20, 24, 473.

Kotler, P. (2000) *Marketing Management*, 10th edn, Prentice-Hall, Englewood Cliffs, NJ.

Kotler, P. (2003) *Marketing Management*, 11th edn, Prentice-Hall, Englewood Cliffs, NJ.

Kotler, P. and Andreasen, A.R. (1991) *Strategic Marketing for Non-Profit Organisations*, Prentice-Hall, Englewood Cliffs, NJ.

Kotler, P. and Armstrong, G. (1996) *Principles of Marketing*, 7th edn, Prentice-Hall, Englewood Cliffs, NJ.

Krastev, S. (1967) 'Marketing of Exported Consumer Products', *Proceedings of SIFT*, Sofia, p.18.

Krastev, S. (1977) 'Foreign Trade Organizations Market Policy', *Journal of Foreign Trade*, Nos 7 and 8, Sofia.

Lasserre, P. and Schutte, H (1999) *Strategies for Asia Pacific Beyond the Crisis*, London, Macmillan.

Lavidge, R.J. (1970) 'The Growing Responsibilities of Marketing', *Journal of Marketing*, Vol. 34 (January), pp.25–8.

Lazer, W. (1969) 'Marketing's Changing Social Relationships', *Journal of Marketing*, Vol. 33 (January), pp.3–9.

Lee, J.R. (2000) *LG Electronics' Overseas Management Success Knowhow*, Muyourk-kyungyong-sa, Seoul.

Lee, S.H. (2001) 'Dimchai's Success Story', *The Weekly Economist*, 25 December.

Levitt, T. (1960) 'Marketing Myopia', *Harvard Business Review*, July/August.

Lévy-Leboyer, M. (1980) 'The Large Corporation in Modern France', in A.D. Chandler and H. Daems, *Managerial Hierarchies, Comparative Perspectives on the Rise of the Modern Industrial Enterprise*, Harvard University Press, Boston, MA; pp.123–45.

Lewis, B.R. (1991) 'Customer Care in Service Organisations', *Management Decision*, Vol. 29, No. 1, pp.31–4.

Lewis, B.R. and Entwistle, T. (1990) 'Managing the Service Encounter: A Focus on the Employee', *International Journal of Service Industry Management*, Vol. 1, No. 3, pp.41–52.

Lewis, R.C. (1989) 'Hospitality Marketing: The Internal Approach', *Cornell Hotel and Restaurant Administration Quarterly*, Vol. 30, Part 3, pp.41–5.

LG Electronics (1995) *Innovation Material 1*, LG Electronics, Korea.

McCarthy, M. (2002) 'US Health-care Inflation Accelerates, According to Government Report', *Lancet*, Vol. 358, No. 9302, p.240.

Mackintosh, J. (2002) 'Halifax Sorry for Snub to "Cash Heavy" Businesses', *Financial Times*, 27 February.

Malaysia (2001) *Eighth Malaysia Plan*, Percetakan Nasional Berhad, Kuala Lumpur.

Mando Company Brochure (2002) Mando, Korea.

Maneva, E. (1984) 'Marketing of Machine-Tools and Turnkey Projects in the Developing Countries', *Proceedings of the Conference on Marketing of Machine-Tools, Electronics and Equipment for the Third World Markets*, Sofia, pp.48–53.

Marinova, E. (1992) *Marketing – Product, Advertising*, Princeps, Sofia.

Marinova, E. (1996) *Marketing Plan*, Princeps, Sofia.

Marsh, H. (2001) 'Dig Deeper into the Database Goldmine', *Marketing*, 11 January, pp.29–30.

Mason, J. (1996) *Qualitative Researching*, Sage, London.

Meek, C. (2002) Personal correspondence with Virtual Spectator Executive Vice President, Business Development.

Meuleau, M. (1988) 'L'introduction du marketing dans l'entreprise en France (1880–1973)', *Revue Française de Gestion*, No. 70, pp.58–71.

Ministry of Commerce (1998) *Electronic Commerce – The Freezer Ship of the 21st Century*, Ministry of Commerce, Wellington.

Mitchell, A. (2001a) 'Playing Cat and Mouse Games with Marketing', *Precision Marketing*, 16 March, p.14.

Mitchell, A. (2001b) 'The End of the Hype', *Marketing Business*, November, p.15.

Mladenova, G. (1998) *Strategic Marketing Planning*, Economy University Publishing Co, Sofia.

National Statistical Institute (1994) *Statistical Reference Book of Republic of Bulgaria*, Statistical Publishing and Printing, Sofia, pp.88–94.

Nayga, R.M. (1994) 'NZ's Statutory Marketing Boards: Recent Developments and Issues', *Agribusiness*, Vol. 10, No. 1, pp.83–93.

New Zealand Newspapers Association (2001) 'Southern Cross Retains Aetna Customers', On-line database accessed via www.stuff.co.nz. Accessed 15 February 2002.

New Zealand Press Association (2002) 'Southern Cross Pays own Hospitals on Time', On-line database accessed via www.stuff.co.nz. Accessed 15 February 2002.

Nikiel, C. (2001) 'Virtual Spectator Breaks into Music Industry On Line', *The National Business Review*, 28 September, On-line edition accessed via www.stuff.co.nz. Accessed 15 February 2002.

Oh, S.R. (1963) *Marketing Principles*, Pakyoung-Sa, Seoul.

O'Malley, L., Patterson, M. and Evans, M. (1999) *Exploring Direct Marketing*, Thomson, London.

O'Malley, L. and Tynan, C. (1999) 'A Reappraisal of Relationship Marketing', *Journal of Marketing Management*, Vol. 15, No. 3, pp.167–78.

O'Sullivan, F. and Gifford, A. (2002) 'The Health Insurance Diamond that Lost its Sparkle', *NZ Herald*, 23 January, On-line edition accessed 15 February 2002.

Palmer, A. (1994) *Principles of Services Marketing*, McGraw-Hill, London; pp.43, 195, 211.

Parker, G. (1999) 'Tories Accused of GM Foods Scaremongering', *Financial Times*, 4 February, p.8.

Perreault, W.D. and McCarthy, E.J. (1999) *Basic Marketing. A Global-Managerial Approach*, McGraw-Hill, Boston, MA.

Pfau, B., Detzel, D. and Geller, A. (1991) 'Satisfy Your Internal Customers', *The Journal of Business Strategy*, November–December, pp.9–13.

Piercy, N. and Morgan, N. (1990) 'Internal Marketing: Making Marketing Happen', *Marketing Intelligence and Planning*, Vol. 8, No. 1, pp.4–6.

Pras, B. (1999) 'Les paradoxes du marketing', *Revue Française de Gestion*, No. 125, pp.99–111.

Precision Marketing (2001–2) Headlines, p.1 in all cases.

Raghavan, S. (2002) 'CRM – Time for Auto Makers to Get Serious', *The Star Business*, 14 March, p.10.

Rajan, Saxena (2002) New Delhi, 'Jet Airways' (A case study), *Marketing Management*, 2nd edn, McGraw-Hill, 616–624.

Ries, A. and Trout, J. (1979) *Positioning*, NTC Business Press, Chicago.

Samiee, S. (1998) 'The Internet and International Marketing: Is There a Fit?', *Journal of Interactive Marketing*, Vol. 12, No. 4 (Autumn), pp.5–21.

Sangameshwaran, P. (2002) 'Second Thoughts On the Indian Consumers', *Indian Management,* April, pp.54–8.

Schultz, D.E. and Kitchen, P.J. (2000) *Global Communications: An Integrated Marketing Approach,* Macmillan Business, Basingstoke.

Schultz, D., Tannenbaum, S. and Lauterborn, R. (1993) *The New Marketing Paradigm,* NTC Business Books, Lincolnwood, IL.

Shapiro, S. and Walle, A.H. (eds) (1987) *Marketing: A Return to the Broader Dimensions,* American Marketing Association, Chicago, IL.

Sharp, A. (1994) *Leap into the Dark: The Changing Role of the State in New Zealand since 1984,* Auckland University Press, Auckland.

Sheeran, G. (2002) 'Health Insurer Likely to up Rates', *Sunday Star Times,* 3 February, On-line edition accessed via www.stuff.co.nz. Accessed 15 February 2002.

Sheth, G., Gardner, D.M. and Garrett, D.E. (1988) *Marketing Theory: Evolution and Evaluation,* John Wiley, New York.

Shick, A. (1998) 'Why Most Developing Countries Should not Try New Zealand's Reforms', *The World Bank Observer,* Vol. 13, No. 1, pp.123–31.

Shubik, M. (1967) 'Information, Rationality and Free Choice in a Future Democratic Society', *Daedalus,* Vol. 96, pp.771–8.

Sidhu, J.S. (2001) 'Different Systems not the Main Challenge', *The Star Business,* 29 June, p.9.

Spector, M. (1999) 'Cracking the Norse Code', *Sunday Times Magazine,* 21 March, pp.45–52.

Stannard, H. (1999) reported in Anonymous, 'UK Perspectives Air Photographic Census', *Precision Marketing,* 24 May, p.5.

Star, The (2001) 'Most Asian Bank Customers Prefer the Personal Touch', *The Star Business,* 18 August, p.7

Statistics New Zealand (2001) *New Zealand Population Statistics.* Statistics New Zealand, Government Printer, Wellington.

Stevenson, P. (2001) 'Row Grows Over Who Pays $50 million ENZA Debt', *NZ Herald.* On-line edition www.nzherald.co.nz. Accessed 4 July 2001.

Strauss, A.L. and Corbin, J. (1990) *Basics of Qualitative Research: Grounded Theory Procedures and Techniques,* Sage, CA.

Talbot, J. (2002) 'Southern Cross Clients Stray', *The Dominion,* 25 January, On-line edition accessed via www.stuff.co.nz. Accessed 15 February 2002.

TATA Statistical Outline of India 2000–2001. www.tata.com/0 economic/ stats outline 2001-02.htm.

Thurow, L.C. (1997) *Towards a High Wage, High Productivity Service Sector,* Economics Policy Unit, Washington, DC.

Todorov, M. (1984) 'PR and Advertising in the Export of Machine-Tools in the Developing Markets', *Proceedings of the Conference on Marketing of Machine-Tools, Electronics and Equipment for the Third World Markets,* Sofia, pp.38–41.

Trade Partners, UK. www.tradepartners.gov.uk.

Triantafyllides, S.A. (1999) 'Banking: Prospects and Challenges for the New Millennium', in *The Cyprus Business Guide,* T & T Publishing, Cyprus; pp.51–3.

Varey, R.J. and Lewis, B.R. (1999) 'A Broadened Conception of Internal Marketing', *European Journal of Marketing,* Vol. 33, Nos 9/10, pp.926–44.

Vassilev, D., Micheva, E., Boeva, B., Petkov, K., Panev, S., Uzunova, Y. and Stanev, D. (1981) *Marketing Theory and Practice*, Nauka I Izkustvo, Sofia.

Weir, J. (2001) 'Health Insurance Cost Doubles in 10 Years', *The Dominion*, 30 November, On-line edition accessed via www.stuff.co.nz. Accessed 15 February 2002.

Whalen, B. (1984) 'Kotler: Rethink the Marketing Concept', *Marketing News*, Chicago, Vol. 18, No. 19, p.3.

Whittington, R. (1999) *Rethinking Marketing*, Sage, London.

Wittgenstein, L. (1921) 'Logisch-philosophische Abhandlung', *Annalen der Naturphilodophie*, Vol. 14, No. 3, pp.4–245.

Wood, J. (1998) 'Mail Marketing Group to Share Leads with US Firm', *Precision Marketing*, 15 June, p.6.

Zeithaml, V.A. and Bitner, M.J. (1996) *Services Marketing*, McGraw-Hill, Singapore, pp.22–3, 304–5, 316, 318, 322–3, 328–9.

Zinkhan, G.M. and Herscheim, R. (1992) 'Truth in Marketing Theory and Research: An Alternative Perspective', *Journal of Marketing*, Vol. 56 (Spring), pp.80–8.

Index

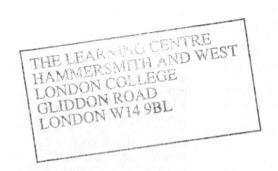